D0938235

HOW GLOBALIZATION SPURS TERRORISM

Praeger Security International Advisory Board

Board Cochairs

Loch K. Johnson, Regents Professor of Public and International Affairs, School of
Public and International Affairs, University of Georgia (U.S.A.)

Paul Wilkinson, Professor of International Relations and Chairman of the Advisory
Board, Centre for the Study of Terrorism and Political Violence, University of
St. Andrews (U.K.)

Members

Anthony H. Cordesman, Arleigh A. Burke Chair in Strategy, Center for Strategic
and International Studies (U.S.A.)

Thérèse Delpech, Director of Strategic Affairs, Atomic Energy Commission, and
Senior Research Fellow, CERI (Foundation Nationale des Sciences Politiques),
Paris (France)

Sir Michael Howard, former Chichele Professor of the History of War and Regis
Professor of Modern History, Oxford University, and Robert A. Lovett Professor of
Military and Naval History, Yale University (U.K.)

Lieutenant General Claudia J. Kennedy, USA (Ret.), former Deputy Chief of Staff
for Intelligence, Department of the Army (U.S.A.)

Paul M. Kennedy, J. Richardson Dilworth Professor of History and Director,
International Security Studies, Yale University (U.S.A.)

Robert J. O'Neill, former Chichele Professor of the History of War, All Souls
College, Oxford University (Australia)

Shibley Telhami, Anwar Sadat Chair for Peace and Development, Department of
Government and Politics, University of Maryland (U.S.A.)

Fareed Zakaria, Editor, *Newsweek International* (U.S.A.)

HOW GLOBALIZATION SPURS TERRORISM

The Lopsided Benefits of "One World" and Why That Fuels Violence

Fathali M. Moghaddam

PRAEGER SECURITY INTERNATIONAL
Westport, Connecticut • London

Library of Congress Cataloging-in-Publication Data

Moghaddam, Fathali M.
How globalization spurs terrorism : the lopsided benefits of "one world" and why
that fuels violence / Fathali M. Moghaddam.
      p.   cm.
   Includes bibliographical references and index.
   ISBN-13: 978-0-313-34480-0 (alk. paper)
   1. Terrorism—Religious aspects—Islam.   2. Terrorism and globalization.
3. Islamic fundamentalism.   I. Title.
   BP190.5.T47M64   2008
   363.325′11—dc22   2008016466

British Library Cataloguing in Publication Data is available.

Copyright © 2008 by Fathali M. Moghaddam

All rights reserved. No portion of this book may be
reproduced, by any process or technique, without the
express written consent of the publisher.

Library of Congress Catalog Card Number: 2008016466
ISBN-13: 978-0-313-34480-0

First published in 2008

Praeger Security International, 88 Post Road West, Westport, CT 06881
An imprint of Greenwood Publishing Group, Inc.
www.praeger.com

Printed in the United States of America

The paper used in this book complies with the
Permanent Paper Standard issued by the National
Information Standards Organization (Z39.48–1984).

10 9 8 7 6 5 4 3 2 1

*This book is dedicated to the Parents Circle,
Families in Israel and Palestine who have lost
immediate family members in the ongoing
conflict and who are building on their
shared grief a hopeful path to peace*

CONTENTS

PREFACE

This book is about how globalization[1] is taking place in a "fractured" manner and resulting in terrorism. I use the term fractured globalization to mean that as economic and technological forces push us toward the global, psychological needs pull us toward the local; as economic barriers weaken and dissolve, identity barriers[2] loom up and become more rigid; as nation states join larger regional unions and we move in some ways closer to a global village, identity-based differences and particularly religious divisions magnify and we become in other ways more balkanized and more separated from one another. It is in the wider context of fractured globalization that we can better understand radicalization and terrorism associated with Islamic communities around the world. Such an understanding requires a macro, long-term view of human societies.

Another important consequence of fractured globalization I explore is a new global American dilemma. The first American dilemma arose out of contradictions between the rhetoric of equality, emanating from the Declaration of American Independence (1776) and other foundational American documents, and the practice of racial segregation. This dilemma was eventually resolved through desegregation legislation and changes in race relations from the 1960s. The new global American dilemma is rooted in contradictions between American ideals and rhetoric in support of democracy around the world, and U.S. government practices in support of "pro-American" dictatorships. The new global American dilemma was brought to a climax during the presidency of George W. Bush (2000–2008), when he authorized the invasion of Iraq as part of a "pro- democracy" agenda, and at the same time continued to support dictatorships in Saudi Arabia, Pakistan, Egypt, and elsewhere in the Near and Middle East. Bush did not create the new global American dilemma, but he brought it to the boil.

The threat of terrorism might serve as a means by which to divert attention away from the new global American dilemma, in part because terrorism seems to demand immediate reactions from U.S. authorities. Of course, it is natural that our immediate reactions to the threat of terrorism have been short term, often very short term—a matter of only days and weeks. Each terrorist threat or actual attack has been followed by frenzied activities on the part of counterterrorist agencies and multiple national and international organizations, focused on trying to deal with the immediate threat, by capturing or destroying the attackers. The media spotlight and the attention of politicians put pressure on everyone involved in counterterrorism to show immediate results. Too often, our understanding of terrorism is shaped by one frantic media event after another, all focused on short-term goals.

While it is imperative and that we have strong short-term counterterrorism strategies that work, and that we "take out" terrorists and foil their plots on a day-to-day basis, it is even more essential that we develop effective long-term policies to end terrorism. In order for such policies to emerge, we must first come to better understand the relationship between terrorism and globalization, "the accelerated integration of capital, production and markets."[3] Such an understanding will enable us to discover the deeper roots of terrorism.

My focus is on terrorism arising from Islamic communities in non-Western and Western societies. This is not because other kinds of terrorism have ended, but because for the next few decades the greatest international threat will remain that of terrorism perpetrated by Islamic fanatics. The rapid growth of Muslim communities in western societies makes this threat more urgent and complicated, in part because it seems so unlikely—as unlikely as specialist medical doctors, who are sworn to protect life, launching terrorist attacks intended to kill civilians, as happened in the United Kingdom in July 2007.

But the so-called "war on terror" will only serve as a short-term distraction from the new global American dilemma. Inevitably, the contradictions between American rhetoric and practices, rhetorical support for democracy and practical support for dictatorships, are bringing into focus the new global American dilemma. How successfully this challenge is tackled has the greatest implications not only for the United States, but also for all humankind.

CHAPTER 1

A Dangerous New World

There are moments in the history of a nation when all that has passed and all that is to come, everything before and after, are forever changed, never to be the same again. This was such a moment for Iran, this was such a time for Iranians, and I was there as a participant. It was the glorious spring of 1979 and along with tens of thousands of other jubilant Iranians I had rushed back from the West to hurl myself into the turbulent currents of fast-moving life in post-revolution Iran, giddy and amazed at the wondrous changes swirling around us.

What contagious excitement! What soaring ambitions and lofty hopes had suddenly sprung to life! We were experiencing the first exhilarating months after the miraculous revolution that had just toppled the Shah, the "king of kings," who we dreamed would be the last in a long line of dictators that cast their hideous shadows far back on Iranian history.[1] Freedom had arrived, so we believed, and we shouted "Freedom!" to one another and to the world.

Casting a cold eye back over the tragic three decades of bloody events in Iran since that tumultuous revolution—the politically motivated murders, the cruel imprisonments and torture, the suffocating spread of a culture of terror, and the emergence of a crushing dictatorship shaped by Islamic fundamentalism—it is difficult to believe how joyous and optimistic we had felt, women and men, in the sublime "spring of revolution." The anguish of the last three decades has almost blotted out the exhilarating hopes we had experienced in that time of innocent bliss.

So many significant incidents come to my mind when I remember that rapturous time, incidents that should have told us of the crushing failures to come. In hindsight it might seem that we, the feverishly inspired youth of that era, giddy with optimism, were wrong to have had such blind faith in the future. We dared to hope that with one frenzied leap we would escape the long, dark tradition of blind obedience to an all-powerful male demagog, and not simply replace the turban for the crown,[2] exchange a dictator Ayatollah for a dictator Shah.

I remember one particularly fine day during that first spring, standing with a leisurely crowd of perhaps two thousand people, listening to political speeches on the grounds of Tehran University, which is located in the center of Tehran, the overcrowded[3] capital city of Iran. The speakers presented a range of "pro-democracy" political positions. The crowd, consisting mostly of students, was in good humor and readily laughed when one of the overly earnest speakers attempted a joke. We, who had witnessed a revolution in the world outside and assumed that there had also been a revolution within each of us, seemed ready to imagine the best about one another, to take our outward show and slogans as revealing changes in the deeper worlds within us. Moreover, why should we not assume so? After all, so much had formally changed in politics and the economy, and the army and security apparatus was in complete disarray. Surely these vast, macro-level changes meant that at the micro level of personal behavior, also, we had changed. Surely this meant a bright future for us.

But as if to dash my hopes, a sinister shadow steadily crept over the sun-drenched gathering that day. I became aware of a dark mob forming at the back of the crowd, and when I looked toward the bustling street outside the university gates, I saw hordes of bearded men climbing out of buses, many of them wearing black shirts. Some of them were carrying banners on sticks, but some others wielded sticks with no banners on them.

A harsh chant rose up from the back of the crowd, becoming louder as more bearded men ran onto the campus and hurled themselves into the now turbulent throng behind us,

> Only one party, Hezbollah![4]
> Only one leader, Ruhollah!
> Only one party, Hezbollah!
> Only one leader, Ruhollah!

The rhythmic chanting grew louder and the rising wave after wave of pressure from the back became stronger, rippling through the crowd and forcing us to jostle forward. At the front of the crowd where I was, we shouted for the pushing to stop and maneuvered nervously, trying to shrug off the intrusion with panache. The volume of the loudspeaker system was increased, so for a while we could still hear the now anxious speaker above the chanting mob that was pushing behind.

A shrill whistle sounded and, as if on a signal, the chanting mass of black shirts swirled forward and attacked, hitting out with clubs as well as chains, knives, and other weapons they had hidden from view as they had slipped onto the university campus. The scene was instantly transformed and we in the crowd now feared for our lives. Primitive instincts took over and our legs carried us faster than I had thought possible.

Those of us at the front were furthest away from the attackers and managed to escape with least injuries. Among the people at the back, there were broken bones and much blood spilled. It seemed like a long time passed before the police and ambulances finally arrived on the scene. By then, the chanting mob of black shirts had been transported away by the same buses that had brought them, but many women and men now lay bloodied and scattered around the university grounds, like broken, discarded dolls. The chanting had been replaced by sirens and the cries and groans of injured people.

To this day, however, the repeated chanting of that frenzied mob still rings in my ears:

> Only one party, Hezbollah!
> Only one leader, Ruhollah!
> Only one party, Hezbollah!
> Only one leader, Ruhollah!

What did they want these club wielders?
What did their rhythmic chants mean?

The fanatical club wielders in Tehran wanted what all religious fundamentalists[5] want, including Christian and Jewish fundamentalists, absolute obedience by everyone to their ideology, and only their ideology, and to their leader, only their leader. Muslim fundamentalists[6] believe exactly what Christian and Jewish fundamentalists believe,[7] that those faithful to their particular religion, and only to their religion, will go to heaven, and those faithful to other religions are damned to go to hell, and must be sent there as soon as possible.

"Hezbollah" literally translated means "party of God," The Muslim fundamentalists in Iran wanted to make sure that the "party of God" would be the one and only political party still standing and active after the revolution. They were ready to injure, maim, and kill, and they did so again and again, to throttle their critics and thwart progress toward a multiparty system. Their goal was to put an end to all debates and to silence dissenting voices.

When the one true path is already known, why tolerate political parties that advocate incorrect alternatives and dedicate themselves to misleading ordinary people down ruinous paths? When the one and only true path of God is clearly visible, why allow atheists, humanists, environmentalists, feminists, communists, liberals, democrats, and other ungodly people locked in unholy alliances to propagate alternative paths?

Only one leader, Ruhollah!

"Ruhollah" is the first name of Ayatollah Khomeini[8] (1900–1989), the religious leader who opposed the Shah, took up residence in exile in Iraq and then France, and returned to Iran in triumph in 1978. The Islamic fundamentalists in Iran were adamant that Ayatollah Khomeini must be unquestioningly accepted by everyone as the unchallenged leader, and all individuals and groups must choose to obey him—or else!

When the one and only qualified leader is clearly recognized by those who are righteous and faithful, why tolerate others who try to mislead the people, the gullible sheep?

The Islamic fundamentalists, like Christian and Jewish fundamentalists, are resolutely against democracy. For them, the people are like a flock of sheep, and it is the duty of the true shepherd to protect and guide the sheep on the right path.

How can we ask the people to vote and to make decisions about the paths society should be taking—why, it would be like allowing a flock of sheep to choose their own way around this extremely dangerous wilderness, planet earth. The sheep would soon wonder off in the wrong direction and get into trouble. From the point of view of fundamentalists, the ills of society, the crime and corruption, arise in large part from basing public policy on the misguided wishes of the people, the dumb, foolish sheep.

THE PEOPLE AS GULLIBLE SHEEP

This tendency to see the people as gullible sheep is present among some circles in all societies, even democracies, and becomes stronger in times of crisis and external threat. For example, during the 1920s and 1930s in western Europe, and again during the 1950s "cold war era," and immediately after 9/11 during the so-called "war on terror" in the United States, there was a tangible move to end civil liberties and to hand power over to a stronger central government. Kazuo Ishiguro[9] brilliantly captures this tendency in his novel *The Remains of the Day*, depicting life in Darlington Hall, near Oxford, England, set mostly during the period between World Wars I and II. This was an era of deep economic and political crisis in western Europe, in circumstances when fundamentalist movements gained ground in many western countries, including in England, where Sir Oswald Mosley (1896–1980) and his "Black Shirts," akin to Adolf Hitler's (1889–1945) brown Shirts, were on the march.

In Ishiguro's novel, Lord Darlington, the head of Darlington Hall, explains to Mr. Stevens, his butler, that in the complicated world of today, we should not expect the man on the street to know enough about economics, politics, trade, and so on, to be able to make correct decisions. The challenges of today are perplexing and enormous, and democracy is no longer a viable solution. In fact, the era of democracy has passed. The best solutions are to be found by an informed elite, those few who really know what is going on in the world. According to Lord Darlington, Germany and Italy put their houses in order by handing over power and trust to Hitler and Benito Mussolini (1883–1945)—the "few who really know."

In the United States during the 1950s, fundamentalists wanted to concentrate power in the hands of General Joseph McCarthy (1909–1957) and others leading the anti-communist crusade. The same fundamentalist tendencies emerged in the United States after 9/11, with a push to concentrate power in the hands of the President George W. Bush, Vice President Cheney, Attorney General Gonzales, and others. This led to warnings by some commentators on the American scene that dictatorship is a real danger for the nation, and that "it could happen here."[10]

But despite the dire warnings about impending dictatorships in western democracies, religious fundamentalism has so far failed to achieve a power monopoly in these societies, in large part because of the contemporary weakness of religiosity in Europe and the traditional separation of church and state in the United States (although this separation will once again be tested in the Supreme Court led by Chief Justice Roberts). This is not the case in Iran, where after the revolution the church and the state became the same thing, and Islamic fundamentalists moved to make their extremist interpretations of the Koran the formal basis of government policy.

Why allow the people to choose the wrong path, when the directions society should take are already spelled out in the Koran? (Christian and Jewish fundamentalists make the same claim about the truth being spelled out in the Bible and the Tora, respectively.) Obviously, the qualified leader should interpret the Koran for the rest of society and illuminate the correct path. Just as obviously, we must not permit anyone else, any of the sheep, to challenge the directives of the qualified leader, the infallible shepherd.

Among Iranian fundamentalists, Ayatollah Khomeini was accepted as an infallible leader, a representative of the "absent Imam" on this earth, this transient and worthless material world. The fundamentalists told us that we "sheep" must do our duty and follow the exalted shepherd, rather than make trouble for ourselves by insisting that our views matter, and that we have a right to explore alternative paths.

No, sheep, this will not do, they said, there must be only one party, Hezbollah, and only one leader, Ruhollah.

There is nothing extraordinary about Islamic fundamentalists; everything they say is echoed by the equally shrill voices of Christian and Jewish fundamentalists. However, there is something extraordinary about, first, the impact of globalization on Muslim fundamentalists and, second, the impact of Muslim fundamentalism on the newly emerging global village.

THE MANY FACES OF GLOBALIZATION

Globalization has many different faces, and is seen very differently in different parts of the world.[11] I am writing this chapter in Malaysia, a multiethnic Muslim country that celebrated its fiftieth year of nationhood in January 2007. Malaysians are proud of their diverse ethnic heritages and languages. How much of this heritage will survive the onslaught of globalization? And what of the situation of practicing Muslims in Malaysia and other Muslim countries? What will become of the Islamic veil worn by traditional Muslim women in the face of international publicity that presents a very different, "liberated" image of the ideal woman? What of the thirty-four or so languages still spoken in Malaysia, how many will still be thriving by the end of the twenty-first century? The answers to these questions remain unknown, although the threat posed by globalization is well known to traditionalists in Malaysia.

From the perspective of Malaysia and other non-western countries, globalization presents real threats to their traditional identities and ways of life. The stronger they value and are tied to their traditional identities and ways of life, the more willing they are to defend their traditional identities against external threat. For Muslim fundamentalists, the threat posed by globalization is terrifying and immediate, and they feel they must defend their traditional heritage against this gigantic global force.

Westerners also feel threatened by globalization; and this perceived threat is not limited just to the economic arena. Of course, so far Americans are more likely to complain about the flood of Chinese products into their markets, rather than the flood of Chinese culture. At social gatherings, at political events, in newspapers, on television, in school and university debates, just about everywhere, Americans in particular are talking about the loss of jobs—either through outsourcing, when the job is exported overseas, or through "real Americans" losing jobs to cheaper imported labor. However, globalization has also resulted in a retrenchment among Americans, a genuine concern about their national identity. One sign of this is the growth of the *English Only Movement*, intended to establish English as the official language of the United States. As Americans feel greater pressure from globalization and the influx of Hispanic immigrants, numbering about 45 million in 2008, there will be increased support for American nationalism and the English Only Movement.[12]

In the European Union, also, local and national identities are strengthening rather than declining as a result of globalization.[13] Already within the framework of the European Union, all kinds of local identities are thriving and being reconstructed, and local traditions are being revived and even manufactured in a rewriting of history. People who were dissolving away when left to themselves are once again defining their differentness, their distinct identities, when directly confronted with other groups. The Welsh are insisting on Welsh names for their city streets, and the Scots are celebrating their local national identity, and language groups in Belgium and Spain and many other places are mobilizing and seeking separatism and distinctiveness, rather than melting away into a global village. Globalization is reviving local identities.

Despite the perceived identity threat, globalization in western societies continues to be primarily an economic threat. The loss of jobs to outsourcing and to "cheap imported labor" remains the primary concerns of Europeans and North Americans. For people in non-western societies, the experience of globalization is fundamentally different.[14]

Because they have less power and influence at the global level, it is people in non-western countries that feel particularly threatened by the impact of globalization. This impact has become extraordinary because of the ways in which the global village is actually becoming a reality.

The Mirage and Reality of Globalization

Received wisdom tells us that globalization means the spread of democracy, and a decline in *ethnocentrism*,[15] the biased tendency to view the characteristics of one's own group as correct and superior to that of out-groups. Received wisdom tells us that the emergence of an interconnected "global village" will strengthen secular, liberal voices, and make for more "openness" and mutual understanding between different people around the world. Received wisdom even predicts an "end to history" as democratic, free-market societies become the norm around the world.

But the indications are that received wisdom is wrong about the consequences of globalization, very wrong. The utopia imagined by some globalization enthusiasts remains promising,[16] in theory at least, but in the meantime we are faced with major challenges and even catastrophes because of the state of affairs in the actual world.

First, globalization is not proving to be a smooth, cohesive process. In practice, we are experiencing *fractured globalization*, the tendency for sociocultural disintegration to pull in a local direction at the same time that macroeconomic and political systems are set up to pull toward the international direction and to accelerate globalization. Fractured globalization involves uneven, sometimes paradoxical, and conflict-ridden changes, with economic–political forces on the one hand, and psychological–cultural forces on the other hand, pulling in different and even diametrically opposite directions.

Second, a consequence of fractured globalization is the strengthening and revival of ethnocentrism,[17] fundamentalism, support for authoritarianism, and a decline in support for the open society.[18] These processes are taking place at a rapid pace, in changes that directly link domestic politics in North America, Europe, China, India, the Middle East, and the rest of the world.

The most important paradox underlying these changes involves the oppositional path of economic and psychological needs. On the one hand, economic forces push toward the creation of larger and larger financial units and corporations spread around the world. Larger and larger companies are gobbling up smaller companies and cornering larger and larger sectors of the global market. But, on the other hand, this economically driven push to become larger is contradicted by a psychological need for people to continue to identify with smaller and local units. After all, it is within the smaller units that individuals have meaningful face-to-face interactions and actual relationships in their everyday lives.

We are moving along two independent and sometimes contradictory paths, captured by the phrase *global economies, local identities*, the economic pull toward the global and the competing, and in some respects stronger psychological pull toward the local. This tension is at the heart of many violent and fanatical movements, including Islamic fundamentalism.

Identity and Islamic Fundamentalism

The Islamic fundamentalists who so aggressively grabbed power after the 1978 revolution in Iran were reaffirming their local, heritage identity and emphatically rejecting the pull of globalization. These fundamentalists saw the importation of foreign (mainly western) values and beliefs, including through the influence of western-trained "experts" such as me, as a serious threat. Democracy, human rights, the "liberation" of women and minorities, and so forth, these were all Satanic threats the fundamentalists saw in the modernized sector of Iran, particularly the universities (modeled, as they were, on western universities). Consequently, a year after the revolution, when the fundamentalists had gained the upper hand in the power struggle against democratic forces, the "Islamic leadership" in Iran launched the so-called "cultural revolution," which involved closing down the universities and expelling professors and students so that they could be reeducated and reunited with "the people" (this Iranian cultural revolution was remarkably like the Chinese cultural revolution of the late 1960s, whereby an aged leader, Mao in China and Khomeini in Iran, encouraged young students to challenge authority, particularly in universities). Since then, there has been periodic "cleansing" of the universities to ensure that they do not develop an identity and culture that is "un-Islamic."

Although universities and western-influenced intellectuals continue to be of concern to the fundamentalists ruling Iran, by far the most urgent and important of their concerns have been women. Government crackdowns in Iran invariably involve a harsher enforcement of the "Islamic *hejab*" (veil) and Islamic behavior among women in particular. In practice, this means bands of armed female and male "morality police" roaming the streets of Tehran and other major cities, harassing women and arresting any female seen to be failing to live up to Islamic behavior. It is important to ask, why are women the particular target of Islamic fundamentalists? Why has the Islamic veil become such a hot-button issue in Islamic communities around the world?

The veil is an example of a *carrier*, which serves as conveyers of cultural values, as "pegs" on which societies can hang their cherished ideals.[19] For example, in the United States "Old Glory," the national flag serves as a carrier. The U.S. national flag and the Islamic veil, both are, from one perspective, "just pieces of cloth," but from another perspective the U.S. national flag and the Islamic veil are sacred carriers that people are willing to die and kill for. The identity of entire peoples is vested in these "pieces of cloth."

The Islamic veil is a vitally important sacred carrier for Islamic fundamentalists because it carries forward, from one generation to the next, the role of women in Islamic societies, a role that serves as a vital foundation for all Islamic communities. Nothing is more important to the maintenance of traditional Islamic communities than the traditional Islamic role of women. The extremely harsh treatment of women who attempt to step outside the restricted boundaries of their role as defined by Islamic fundamentalists, who for example fail to wear the veil in the "correct" manner, has to be understood in this context.

Carriers such as the Islamic veil and the U.S. national flag serve to sustain and strengthen group identity and cohesion. Such carriers have a vital function in the long-term survival of the group, not just in any shape but also with its essential characteristics intact. Islamic fundamentalists intend to return Islamic societies to their "pure" Islamic form, and not to have Islamic societies become "reformed" and changed in a way that makes them less Islamic. The harsh tactics that some fundamentalists employ, including terrorist attacks of various types (attacking women who fail to wear the veil in the "correct" manner, bombing nightclubs and markets, and other "such centers of corruption") should be seen as a reaction to the perceived threat from an out-group and the fear of collective annihilation.

Identity and Identification in Islamic Communities Around the World

The 1978 revolution in Iran was one of the series of events over the last four decades that have led to an increased identification of Muslims around the world with the label "Muslim." Correspondingly, there has been an increased awareness among non-Muslims of the category "Muslim." Thus, there is both greater collective consciousness among Muslims, and greater consciousness among non-Muslims of Muslims as a group.

This trend represents a move away from the secular nationalism spearheaded by leaders such as by Kamal Abdul Nasser (1918–1970), and Anwar Sadat (1918–1981), whereby collective movements in the Near and Middle East attempted to reject religion as a basis for mass mobilization. Through the revolution in Iran, Ayatollah Khomeini wanted to inspire and rally all Muslims around the world under the banner of Islam. Khomeini's anti-American, antielite, and anticorruption message was highly popular among the poorer sectors of many Muslim societies, particularly in Lebanon and Iraq. However, because Khomeini was a Shi'a Muslim and a Persian, and because the vast majority of Muslims in the Near and Middle East are Sunni Arabs, Arab leaders were able to limit Khomeini's influence by playing up the historic split between Shi'a and Sunni Muslims as well as between Persians and Arabs.[20] The culmination of attempts by Arab leaders to control and ultimately end "Khomeini's revolution" was the 1980–1988 war between Iraq and Iran, in which Saddam Hussein represented Arab Sunni interests against Shi'a Iran.

However, the movement toward raising "Islamic consciousness" had other strands that developed within the majority Sunni populations, Sunnis consisting of about 95 percent of all Muslims in the world. This consciousness rising came about in part through attacks on Muslim lands, including the Soviet invasion of Afghanistan in 1979 and the U.S.-led invasions of Iraq in 1991 and again 2003. These wars allowed Muslim fundamentalists to frame local conflicts, such as those in Afghanistan and Iraq, as being part of a global war between Islam and foreign powers. Of course, the center of this global war is depicted as being the cause of Palestine and the campaign to expel Israeli from "occupied Muslim lands." The unequivocal support for Israel on the part of the United States, as well as the U.S. military presence in various parts of the Near and Middle East, has meant that Muslims who perceive their group to be under attack also view the United States as their main protagonist.

The "Distance Traveled Hypothesis"

Particularly since the 1970s, there has been a gradual growth of Muslim populations in western Europe, and an increasing number of Muslims in Europe identify with the label "Muslim." The rise in "Islamic consciousness" in western Europe has been far more radical than in the United States. The main reason for this difference is explained by reference to what I call *the distance traveled hypothesis*, the greater the distance that immigrants have to travel to reach the adopted country, the more material and intellectual resources they need. As a consequence, for example, immigrants who reach the United States from Asia are more resourceful than immigrants who reach the United States from Mexico. This is reflected in the relatively greater educational and financial success of Asians in the United States compared to Mexicans.

Applying the distance traveled hypothesis to the situation of Muslims in Europe as compared to the United States, we arrive at certain predictable patterns. First, Muslims in Europe are relatively closer in physical proximity to the Islamic heartland and their homes (the countries of North Africa, South Asia, Near and Middle East); Muslim immigrants in North America are further away and find it more difficult to maintain ties to their countries of heritage. Second, because of the relative closeness of Europe and the greater physical distance between the United States and traditional Islamic countries, Muslims with less material and intellectual resources find it easier to move to Europe than to the United States. Whereas in Europe Muslim immigrants are characterized by lower educational and financial achievements (there are several exceptional groups, such as affluent and well-educated Iranians who fled to Europe after the 1978 revolution), in the U.S. Muslim immigrants are characterized by higher educational and financial achievements.

Because Muslims in Europe tend to be lower in social class than Muslims in the United States, and because of the closer physical proximity of Muslims in Europe to their Islamic countries of heritage, the message of radical Islam is having a greater impact on Muslims in Europe. Add to this the advantage the United States has as a historically immigrant receiving society, with the power of the "American Dream" and "anyone can make it in America" ideology, and it becomes clear why "homegrown" Islamic terrorism is a greater threat in Europe than it in the United States.[21] Muslims in western Europe are facing a far more difficult task assimilating into mainstream society, and more likely to identify with the global "Islamic cause."

THE MESSAGE AND PLAN OF THIS BOOK

Western politicians such as Gordon Brown, the Prime Minister of the United Kingdon, may well be correct in predicting that it will take generations to end Islamic terrorism. Through scientific advances, we can now transport people to the moon, unravel the genetic basis of some very complex diseases, build bridges that span miles of water, communicate instantly with others situated anywhere on earth, clone animals, build powerful computers that can defeat even the greatest grandmasters at chess, and succeed in so many other tasks that would have seemed unthinkable just a century ago, but when it comes to understanding and preventing terrorism, we still seem impotent, primitive, ignorant, and powerless. Why is this?

The answer, I argue, is that we have failed to understand the time frame that must be considered in order to explain the current wave of Islamic terrorism. In these discussions, the time frame has been over the course of individual (terrorist) lives. Again and again, attempts have been made to explain terrorism by focusing on psychological processes, related to social, cognitive, and personality characteristics, that span the lives of individuals. For example, it is proposed that terrorists are characterized by certain pathologies ("Terrorists are mad! Absolutely crazy!") or education level ("Terrorists are illiterate and unintelligent!") or economic condition ("Terrorism arises out of poverty!"), or moral commitment ("Terrorists have no morality!"). This approach has major shortcomings.

The Staircase to Terrorism

The reductionist approach (summed up as "the few bad apples" theory) to explaining terrorism has led to a dead end. It is now generally accepted that terrorists are not pathological,[22] low in education, economically poor, or even devoid of morality. Although terrorists are not committed to the morality of mainstream society, they are very strongly committed to their alternative morality. We will not win the "war on terror" by focusing on "a few bad apples" because terrorism arises first and foremost out of certain contexts ("rotten barrels") and the "bad apples" we "take out" will be quickly replaced by other "bad apples" as long as the context remains unchanged. Also, the process of becoming a terrorist is incremental, as the individual is step by step transformed by the "rotten barrel." In order to better capture this picture, I introduced a staircase metaphor for how terrorists take form.

Imagine a building with a staircase, where everyone begins on the ground floor. There are about 1.2 billion Muslims on the ground floor. The most important feature of the situation is how people perceive the building and the options they have on each floor. None of the people on the ground floor think of themselves as terrorists or as supporters of terrorism, but a small number move up to higher floors and eventually some of these individuals become terrorists. As people move up the staircase, the power of the context increases and they find they have fewer and fewer choices in behavioral options. To explain this transition, we need to attend to the distinct psychological processes that characterize each floor on the staircase to terrorism.

On the ground floor, people are particularly concerned with their identities, that is "what kind of person am I? What kind of group do I belong to?"[23] They are motivated to be positively evaluated and to be seen as distinct, as having an identity that is in some ways different. They are also concerned with justice, with being treated fairly. Research shows that the sense of justice is not only dependent on our "rewards" or outcomes (distributive justice), but also on our involvement in the decision-making process (procedural justice). In situations where we feel we have "voice" and we are participants in decision making, we are far more likely to feel we have been treated fairly—even though we might not get a "bigger reward" at the end of the process. In Islamic communities, many people feel they are being treated unfairly, and many experience inadequate identities. Some of these individuals move up the staircase to better their conditions.

On the first floor, individuals search for avenues to achieve social mobility as well as to gain voice in decision making. Nepotism, corruption, and lack of employment and educational opportunities in many Islamic societies of the Near and Middle East mean that individuals who reach the first floor often become more frustrated. About 60 percent of the populations of these societies are under twenty-five years of age, resulting in large numbers of disappointed young people on the first floor. Some of these individuals are motivated enough to seek solutions on the second floor. It is important to emphasize that, as yet, these individuals do not endorse terrorism, nor do they see themselves as terrorists.

The most important psychological process influencing thought and action on the second floor is displacement of aggression. Sigmund Freud (1856–1939) showed brilliant insight in his ground breaking discussions of displacement and intergroup dynamics, showing how groups can maintain in-group cohesion by displacing negative affect onto target out-groups.[24] Freud gave particular importance to the role of the leader in directing negative affect onto out-group targets perceived to be dissimilar. In Islamic countries of the Near and Middle East, and in Islamic communities around the world generally, the tendency has been for leaders (from national leaders to preachers in local mosques) to focus attention onto two external targets: the United States and Israel, or what the Iranian leader Ayatollah Khomeini called "the Great Satan and the Little Satan." In this way, local corruption, ineptitude, poor management, and other shortcomings of the Islamic world are blamed on the United States and Israel, and aggression is directed away from local leadership.

Some individuals move up from the second to the third floor, where they become further engaged in a morality supportive of terrorism. International surveys show that some Muslims (as many as 10–30 percent, depending on the country) in the Near and Middle East, as well as in Muslim communities based in western Europe, now endorse the view that terrorism is justified in order to protect Islam. Again, it is important to emphasize that individuals who reach the third floor do not see themselves as terrorists, nor are they engaging in terrorist acts. However, they have moved one step closer to becoming suitable for recruitment to terrorist networks, because they have adopted a morality that condones terrorism.

The main psychological process characterizing the thoughts and actions of individuals who move up to the fourth floor is categorical thinking and the rigid division of the social world into "us versus them," "good versus evil." Everyone who is in the "them" category becomes a potential target for aggression, because "you are either with us or against us." Unfortunately, this kind of simplistic and dangerous categorical thinking has been further endorsed and mirrored by the rhetoric of some western leaders, particularly during the presidency of George W. Bush (2000–2008). The extremists on the two sides have strengthened one another through their speeches and discourse generally.

From among those individuals who reach the fourth floor, a small number move to the fifth floor and take part in terrorist activities. We tend to use the term 'terrorist' in a broad way, as if everyone involved in terrorism is engaged in the same activities. We tend to overlook the fact that there are many specializations in terrorist networks. Through an assessment of available evidence, I identified nine different branches of specialization, from the 'inspirational leader' who is internationally visible, to strategists, networkers, local agitators and guides, fund raisers, technical 'experts', cell managers, cell members, and 'fodder'— the individuals who engage in the high risk actions, such as suicide terrorism.

The Need to Focus on Long-Term Processes

A second major shift that needs to take place in how we interpret terrorism-concerned time frame, which should be very long term, focusing on evolutionary processes, and not just part of an individual life, as is the traditional approach. This long-term time frame is an integral part of the evolutionary context of terrorism. The main thesis of this book is that terrorism arises out of certain types of intergroup relationships and is a collective defense mechanism, albeit a destructive one, for the survival of minority groups who perceive themselves to be under attack and facing annihilation.

The context of Islamic terrorism is fractured globalization, involving serious tensions, paradoxes, cultural clashes associated with rapid changes in technology and lifestyles, and enormous movements of people, ideas, and goods around the world. In this context, certain groups suddenly find themselves in contact with competitor out-groups and possible extinction, despite being completely unprepared for such contact. The result is a perceived collective threat, a fear of being annihilated as a group, and the rise of ethnocentrism and fundamentalism as the in-group mobilizes to defend its heritage culture and try to survive.

Plan of This Book

In the first part of this book (Chapters 2 to 5), the context of Islamic terrorism is explored. The discussion begins (Chapter 2) with a consideration of how the different schools of thought approach the nature of human nature. After all, terrorists are humans, and how we answer the question "what is a terrorist?" depends on how we first answer the question "what is a human being?" I argue (Chapter 3) that there are a number of universal human needs, such as identity needs. Threats to these needs can result in irrational defensive reactions, including violent ones.

Of course, to understand human beings in the twenty-first century, we must assess human behavior in the context of globalization. From some perspectives, globalization is beneficial and even an ideal path, and we consider this viewpoint in Chapter 4. But globalization also has serious enemies, who believe that globalization changes are bringing about new destruction, inequalities, injustices, victory for the "immoral" groups and extinction for some legitimate groups. This viewpoint is examined in Chapter 5. The final chapter in Part One of the book is an examination of fractured globalization, pointing out some of the paradoxes, tensions, and conflicts that globalization entails. This discussion of fractured globalization sets the stage for Part Two of the book, which focuses on terrorism and catastrophic evolution.

The chapters in Part Two are set in the context of long-term evolutionary changes. Part Two begins with an exploration (in Chapter 6) of what takes place when an in-group is brought into sudden contact with an out-group with little or no preparedness. There is considerable evidence that both among human and nonhuman life forms, sudden contact can result in the sudden decline in numbers, and even extinction, of one or both life forms involved in the interaction. The dramatic decline in diversity in human cultures and languages, as well as among animals and plants, reflects this trend. Because of the enormous complexities of human cultures, the path from sudden contact to decline and extinction is more complex. Understanding this complexity requires closer attention to the particular process of relations between human groups. The unfolding of intergroup relations in the context of catastrophic evolution is discussed in terms of threatened identities (Chapter 7), and rights and duties (Chapter 8).

The new global American dilemma is the focus of chapters in Part Three. First, I articulate the new "global" American dilemma (Chapter 9), one that naturally and inevitably arises from the traditions of the United States, when these traditions are played out on the world stage. To understand the new global American dilemma, we need to think back to the original American dilemma, that is contradictions between American ideals, as captured by the United States *Declaration of Independence* for example, and the practice of slavery inevitably led to the resolution of this contradiction through the American Civil War (1861–1865), and later racial segregation led to the desegregation movement of the 1960s.

The new global American dilemma involves a similar contradiction. The presence of the United States on the world stage as the sole super-power highlights certain contradictions between American ideals and U.S. government foreign policy. The most important example of this contradiction is between the rhetoric of freedom and democracy on the one hand and support for certain corrupt dictatorships on the other hand. As women in the United States become more active in national and international politics, this will further highlight American support for regimes which deny women basic human rights. These contradictions point to the role of irrational unconscious forces in shaping international relations, and particularly the relations between the United States and the so-called "rogue states," such as Iran and Cuba.

In the "Afterward" section, I propose that the key to changing Islamic societies is to reform the role and status of women in these societies, both inside and outside the home. Of course, by "reform" I do not imply that women in Islamic societies must copy women in western societies; however, I do mean that women in Islamic societies must achieve parity in economic, political, social, and cultural spheres. Such a reform would transform relationships both within the family and in the larger society, and it would lead to a revolution in socialization practices and person-ality development in Islamic communities.[25] The reason why Islamic fundamentalists are utterly opposed to reforms in the role and status of women is that they too are aware of this being the key to what happens in the larger community over the long term.

PART ONE

The Global Context of Terrorism

Turning and turning in the windening gyre
The falcon cannot hear the falconer
—William Buttler Yeats[1]

"Now and then it is possible to observe the moral life in process of
revising itself...The news of such an event is often received with
a degree of irony or some other sign of resistance."
—Lionel Trilling[2]

Fractured globalization is associated with major shifts in the global moral
order, as the cultures and value systems of some societies spread and
gain influence, and the cultures and value systems of other societies
decline and lose influence. These changes reflect global transformations,
the passing away of the old order, and the emergence of a new order.
The poet William Butler Yeats conjures up the image of a falcon that
has lost touch with the falconer, indicative of a loss of control at the
center. Somewhere, a new center or, more likely multiple new centers
are emerging.[3]

The global shifts we are experiencing, and particularly the decline
of traditional moral orders, are giving rise to counter movements and
reactions, some of them radical and even violent. Terrorism is just one
example of these counter movements, as violent extremists react to enormous changes they sense, changes that seriously threaten the continua-
tion of lifestyles they support. In an important sense, Islamic terrorists
are fighting for survival, the survival of their moral order.

Islamic fundamentalists have good reason to feel threatened. The vast changes sweeping across the world are associated with transformed social roles, especially for women. The new values of equality, liberation, and freedom associated with the transformed role of women inevitably clash with the values of Islamic fundamentalism. This matters particularly because Islamic fundamentalists, unlike Christian and Jewish fundamentalists, are actually in the business of governing or seriously competing to govern states, as is clear from the situations in Iran, Afghanistan, Pakistan (the first state to officially be declared an Islamic Republic), Saudi Arabia, among other states.

In what ways do Islamic fundamentalists feel threatened? To address this question, we need to dig deeper into basic needs that are shared by all humankind. Of particular interest in this context are needs that are related to identity. We live in an age in which diversity is celebrated, and intergroup differences rather than similarities are a focus of attention. The rhetoric of diversity has led us to ignore the basic needs that we humans all share.

Basic shared human needs, such as identity needs, arise out of the common evolutionary challenges that we share. When the environmental conditions change, as they are changing dramatically through fractured globalization, then the basic needs of at least some groups are threatened. In order to highlight the threats associated with changing environmental conditions, I discuss globalization as an ideal (Chapter 4) in contrast to fractured globalization (Chapter 5). Thus, the four chapters in Part One of this book identify certain universals in human social behavior, explore the difference between globalization as an ideal and globalization as it is actually taking place (fractured globalization), and highlight perceived threats to basic human needs, particularly identity needs, arising from fractured globalization.

CHAPTER 2

The Psychological Citizen and Globalization

Throughout much of the twenty-first century, we have become accustomed to listening to dramatic news about terrorist threats, plots, and bloody attacks, not only in Iraq, Afghanistan, Pakistan, Israel, and other distant lands, but also in the United States, England, Spain, Denmark, and other western societies. Even though such news is now routinely part of our daily media diet, we tend to see the plotters and perpetrators of terrorism as something extraordinary, as inhuman and unnatural. How could it be otherwise? How could a suicide bombing be part of normal human experiences?

However, it is a profound mistake to set terrorist behavior apart from the rest of human behavior, to treat it as being in a completely different category. This is because twenty-first- century Islamic terrorism is extremist behavior that has evolved as part of collective reactions arising out of particular global circumstances, and is explained by the particular nature and extraordinary power of the twenty-first- century human context. Just as the behavior of U.S. military personnel in Abu Ghraib prison is explained by the characteristics and power of the context, rather than the "few bad apples" explanation offered by Donald Rumsfeld and others,[4] terrorism has to be understood as a result of the larger context. Explanations for both torture committed by U.S. military personnel in contexts such as Abu Ghraib prison and terrorism emanating from Islamic communities, are in important ways linked, both rooted in how the behavior of individuals is shaped by context and authority.

MIRROR IMAGES: TERRORISM AND TORTURE

Indeed, at a deeper psychological level, there are profound links between terrorism committed by Islamic fanatics and torture perpetrated at Abu Ghraib and other such locations by U.S. personnel. In both instances, the deeper motivation, rarely acknowledged explicitly, is to humiliate, to shame, and to instill a sense of helplessness—both among the enemy and among the home population. Torture seldom leads to reliable information, but it can make a population feel humiliated and helpless. Indeed, often the deeper reasons why torture is carried out has little to do with information gathering and a great deal to do with, first, intimidating and controlling the enemy population and, second, raising the threat level and increasing cohesion and support for leadership among the in-group population.[5] Similarly, terrorism seldom achieves a material objective, but terrorist acts can instill fear and a strong sense of helplessness and humiliation.

Both torture and terrorism arise out of "rotten barrels" rather than because of a "few bad apples." Of course, even in the most powerful contexts, not everyone will do the "wrong thing." Not all the U.S. military personnel in Abu Ghraib prison took part in torturing Iraqi prisoners, and not all Iraqis trapped in the horrific living conditions of post-2003 Iraq went on to commit terrorist acts. However, because of the power of context, larger numbers of individuals will "do the wrong thing." The relationship between context and behavior can be better understood through the concept of "degrees of freedom," which I discuss next.

DEGREES OF FREEDOM AND BEHAVIOR

Imagine you have been summoned to appear as a witness in a court of law. You enter the courtroom at the appointed day and time, are sworn in by a court official, and take your place in the witness stand. Everyone in court, from the judge and lawyers to the court ushers, guards, and the jury, have to abide by a strict set of rules. How you behave as a witness is severely restricted by the rules of the court. You are not permitted to speak out aloud when you feel like it, or move from the witness stand and walk around the courtroom as you wish. In the middle of the proceedings you might notice something comical about one of the members of the jury or about the judge, or you might suddenly remember a hilarious joke a friend told you about a court case, but you are not permitted to speak about your comical insight or tell the joke to the rest of the court. Your behavior is strictly controlled and you have almost no freedom to deviate from the how you must behave as a witness in court. You are obligated to listen to questions asked by lawyers and the judge, and to answer these questions honestly and directly. If you fail to do this, you will be breaking the law and could receive punishment. This is a situation with low degrees of freedom, meaning that the context of the court of law is strong and to a large extent shapes your behavior. From the moment you step into the court until you leave, your behavior is very restricted.[6]

Now imagine that after giving witness at a court trial, you go with some friends to a county fair. There are all kinds of amusements and games, lots of animals on display, people in wild costumes clowning around and making each other laugh, and a wonderful variety of food to sample. You are free to roam around the fair and to explore the various games and activities in any order that you desire. You are also free to speak when you feel like it and to say almost anything that comes to your mind. Of course, there are also rules that have to be followed at the fair. For example, the games you can play also have rules that you have to follow. But, in general, you have a great deal more freedom to innovate and do things as you "feel like it." This is a situation with greater degrees of freedom, meaning that the context sets fewer restrictions on your behavior.

We can conceive of a continuum with two extremes (see below), with infinite degrees of freedom at one extreme and zero degrees of freedom at the other extreme. All contexts fall on this continuum somewhere between these two extremes, with the court of law toward the zero degrees of freedom end and the county fair closer to the infinite degrees of freedom end.

Zero Degrees of Freedom _____ Infinite degrees of Freedom

Personality Factors and Degrees of Freedom

There exists a direct relationship between the role of personality factors and the degrees of freedom in a context. Understanding this relationship is vital to understanding how radicalization and terrorism evolve to involve greater and smaller numbers of people.

We can summarize the relationship between the role of personality factors and the degrees of freedom in a context in the following way: the lower the degrees of freedom, the less important will be the role of personality in behavior. To express the same idea another way, the greater the degrees of freedom, the more room there is for personality differences to become manifest in behavior. This is a vitally important idea, and so I clarify it further through some examples below.

Imagine a family friend has passed away and you are attending his funeral. You arrive for the funeral ceremony, accompanied by several members of your family. The atmosphere is solemn, as the priest and the funeral officials guide the attendants through the various procedures in the traditional funeral ceremony. You have attended few funeral ceremonies in your life and you are unsure about the procedures, so you pay close attention to what other people are doing and follow along. The participants are silent for the most part, and each speaks softly when it comes to her or his turn to express condolences to the wife and close family of the deceased. In the context of the funeral ceremony, there are few degrees of freedom, meaning that the context is "strong" and has a powerful impact on behavior. As a result, there is little difference in the behavior of the participants; there is little opportunity for personality differences to show themselves in behavior. As a rule, in "strong" contexts there are few degrees of freedom, and the behavior of most people is very similar. That is, personality differences do not have an opportunity to manifest themselves.

Traditional research has assumed that underlying personality are certain traits that are universal and consistent across contexts. Traditional researchers claim to have discovered five such traits, *conscientiousness* (the extent to which a person is responsible/irresponsible), *agreeableness* (the extent to which a person is gentle/rough, good natured/irritable, and so on), *openness to experience* (the extent to which a person is imaginative/simple, curious/unreflective), *extroversion* (the degree to which a person is sociable and outgoing), and *neuroticism* (the degree to which a person is calm/anxious, composed/excitable, and so on).[7] Behavior is assumed to be shaped by the level of agreeableness, conscientiousness, extroversion, openness to experience, and neuroticism. However, even if we accept the assumption that there are such "universal personality traits," the influence of such individual difference variables diminishes greatly in contexts where there are few degrees of freedom.

I argue that Islamic communities are in some important respects increasingly becoming "strong" contexts, where there are fewer degrees of freedom and more people are being pushed to behave in similar ways. This is particularly true of Islamic communities of the Near and Middle East, where cultural, political, economic, and psychological factors are diminishing degrees of freedom for most people. But it is also true of Islamic communities in western Europe, where Muslims are identifying with the plight of Muslims perceived to be under siege in Iraq, Palestine, among other regions.

Identification Strength and Degrees of Freedom

There is an important relationship between identity and degrees of freedom.[8] The stronger an individual identifies with a group, the lower the degrees of freedom for that individual in the group context. Individuals who identify more strongly with Islam also conform more with what they believe to be the correct form of behavior for Muslims. For example, women who identify more strongly with Islam and believe that being a Muslim obligates women to wear the hejab, tend to conform to this norm. In this sense, these female believers experience smaller degrees of freedom in the social context, because their behavior is more strongly regulated by "Islamic norms."

Of course, the concept of degrees of freedom and the emphasis on characteristics of the context should not lead us to neglect the characteristics of individuals. This is because in contexts where the degrees of freedom are high, there is plenty of room for individual personality characteristics to influence behavior. Within such "weak" contexts, it becomes more relevant to ask, what are the personality characteristics of terrorists? But in the present circumstances, Islamic communities, particularly in the Near and Middle East, represent strong rather than weak contexts, there are fewer degrees of freedom for behavior in public contexts. In the crude language of power politics, censorship of various kinds is stronger in these communities.

Performance Capacity And Performance Style

Even in strong contexts where there are few degrees of freedom, are there certain limits to how the context can change human behavior? A useful distinction to introduce here is between *performance capacity*, to do with how well a person can perform a particular task, and *performance style*, the manner in which a task is carried out and the meaning it is ascribed.[9] Consider, for example, a group of cowboys sitting around a camp fire on a dark night. One of the cowboys suddenly stands up, pulls out his gun, and asks, "Did you hear that? What was that sound?" The first question, "Did you hear that" concerns performance capacity. Some of the older cowboys report that they did not hear anything, and the oldest cowboy responds, "You know I'm almost deaf, can't hear nothing." But two of the younger cowboys agree there was a sound, "Yes, we heard it didn't we Geoff?" responds the first one, and "Sure did!" confirms the second.

"But what was it?" asks the oldest cowboy. This is a question concerning performance style, about the meaning of a phenomenon.

"Sounded like a bear to me, better watch out."

"No, that weren't no bear, more like a tree breaking... that makes a groaning sound too... "

"I thought it somebody shouting... "

In assessing how context can influence behavior, the distinction between performance style and performance capacity is crucial, because even a strong context with low degrees of freedom has little or no impact on performance capacity. For example, how well a person's auditory system functions and how well a person hears sounds, are not influenced by context. The hearing ability of the "almost deaf" cowboy would not improve significantly in another context, just as the hearing ability of the younger cowboys would not change significantly with context. However, performance style is fundamentally shaped by context; the meaning a person gives to a sound depends on the situation. If instead of being gathered around a camp fire at night out on the range the cowboys were sitting in a hotel in town, instead of thinking that the sound they heard was a bear, or a tree branch breaking, or a person calling, they might imagine the sounds to be something else completely, such as a train passing by or noise from a saloon.

Thus, we can pin down the question to be addressed more precisely: how malleable is performance style? How much can context influence how things are done and the meanings ascribed to phenomena in the world?

In addressing this question, let me emphasize that I am addressing the question of "human nature" and the characteristics of all human beings, rather than treating terrorists as "a few bad apples," a "unique" set of individuals, who in terms of personality characteristics, have to be considered as part of a completely different category. My proposal, backed by an impressive body of empirical research,[10] is that under certain circumstances psychologically normal people can behave abnormally and do terrible harm to others. Thus, we need to reflect back on ourselves and rethink our own characteristics.

I begin this reflection by examining how human behavior is viewed by the major schools of thought, categorized into following two groups: group one, schools that assume humans come into this world with "fixed," innate characteristics; group two, schools that assume humans arrive in this world as "blank slates" and are subsequently shaped by their experiences. Group one thinkers highlight universals in human behavior, assumed to be the result of inbuilt characteristics; whereas group two highlight diversity and variations in behavior across groups, assumed to be the result of different environmental experiences.

I argue that environmental factors in important ways shape behavior, but that there are also certain important universals. There is no doubt that genetic factors influence universals, but there has been a tendency for researchers to neglect the role of environmental conditions in leading to universals in behavior. Certain common environmental challenges are shared by all humans, and the common human resolution of these challenges results in similarities in behavior across different human groups.

DIFFERENT PERSPECTIVE ON THE PSYCHOLOGICAL CITIZEN

"What a piece of work is a man, how noble in reason, how infinite in faculties, in form and moving how express and admirable, in action how like an angel, in apprehension how like a god: the beauty of the world, the paragon of animals! And yet to me what is this quintessence of dust?"

—*Hamlet* (II, 2, 303–308)

An ancient Sufi story recounts the experiences of a group of blind beggars who were traveling together on foot from town to town. One of the beggars explains that the next town they will reach has the reputation of being home to the elephant, a mysterious animal with very strange characteristics. None of the beggars had ever come across an elephant before, so they decided to go their separate ways during the day around the town and to regroup in the evening. They agreed that during their shared evening meal, they would talk about what each of them had discovered about the elephant. When evening came and they were once again gathered as a group, the first one to speak about the elephant declared triumphantly that he had found one of these mysterious animals and discovered it to be just like a very fat snake. This blind beggar did not realize that he had only managed to get his hands around the trunk of an elephant. The next beggar to speak about the elephant declared just as emphatically that this animal was actually like a big flapping wing covered with very rough skin; he did not understand that he had only touched the ear of an elephant. The next blind beggar to speak had touched only the tail of an elephant, and now he insisted that the elephant is actually like a short rope. The beggars argued all night, claiming the elephant to be like a tree trunk, or a sack of lard, or some other bizarre object. Each blind beggar had touched only a small part of an elephant, and each wrongly supposed that he had understood the whole picture.

The beggars were blind to what the elephant really is, but they were also blind to the perspectives of other individuals in their group. They could not see that if they combined all of their descriptions, they would at least get closer to the truth: one part of the elephant is like a rope, another part is like a tree trunk, another part is like a wing covered with rough skin, another part is like a snake, and so on.

Hamlet does have the ability to see human beings through the eyes of others. He understands that humans can be seen as noble in reason, infinite in faculties, in action like an angel, in apprehension like a god, and so on, but for Hamlet this creature is "the quintessence of dust." In the twenty-first century, narrowly trained specialists offer competing images of what a human is, but they seldom go outside their own specialized niches to appreciate the images offered by other groups of specialists—they are more like the blind beggars than like Hamlet.

The danger is that relying on modern specialists who each focus on a narrow feature of the psychological citizen, we too will make the same mistake as the blind beggars, that we will also touch a small part of the psychological citizen and assume we have arrived at the entire picture. The different schools of psychology present us with rather different images of what this creature is.[11] We need to be careful not to be seduced by any one narrow perspective, any one part of the whole.

One way to assess the contributions of the different schools in an integrated manner is to categorize the schools into following two groups: *group one*, the schools that place more emphasis on the inbuilt characteristics of the psychological citizen; *group two*, the schools that place more emphasis on the shaping of the psychological citizen by the environmental conditions. This classification leads to structuralism, Gestalt psychology, psychoanalysis, cognitive psychology, and evolutionary psychology in group one, and behaviorism and social constructionism in group two.

Group One: The "Fixed" Nature of the Psychological Citizen

From the viewpoint of schools in the first category, the psychological citizen comes into this world with important inbuilt characteristics. These characteristics are shared by all humans and are part of what is generally referred to as "human nature," with the strong implication that such "nature" is unchanging. Also, with respect to how we go about discovering "human nature," from its beginnings, modern psychology was dominated by researchers who assumed they have found the "scientific" methods needed to discover "human nature" (of course, to this day, there is controversy about just what such methods are).

The structuralists, led by Edward Titchener (1867–1927), who was trained by the father of experimental psychology Wilhelm Wundt (1832–1920), were particularly influential in the latter part of the nineteenth century. These researchers worked from the "ground up," on the assumption that the human mind is made up of the basic "elements" of thought (rather like a physical object being made up of chemical elements, but for Titchener mental life is a process). This "atomistic" view leads us to focus on the psychological citizen as a thinker, looking inward and using introspection to accurately report on what goes on inside the mind. An assumption is that we are rational creatures and are capable of being trained to use introspection to discover how and why we think the way we do.

Cognitive neuroscientists working in the twenty-first century also tend to treat the psychological citizen as a thinking machine, but they are far less dependent on introspection and self-reports as a way of getting information about mental processes.[12] The new brain imaging techniques, such as fMRI (functional Magnetic Resonance Imaging), now allow researchers to identify the particular areas of the brain that become more active while a person is engaged in specific mental tasks, such as working on a verbal riddle or a math problem. These contemporary researchers have attempted to identify the specific locations in the brain that are causally linked to particular types of behavior.

The idea that human beings are born with certain inbuilt, "hard wired" characteristics that structure our experiences was central to the viewpoint of Gestalt psychologists, who were particularly influenced in the 1920s and 1930s. For example, Gestalt psychologists demonstrated how our perceptions of the world are influenced by similarity and proximity, so that things that are more similar to one another (e.g., green balls vs. blue balls) and physically closer to one another (children standing next to each other at one end of a playground vs. children standing together in another part of a playground) are more likely to be seen by us as being in two different groups. The links between how we perceive nonsocial phenomena (such as green and blue balls) and social phenomena (such as people of different ethnicities) became better understood through research carried out mostly in England.

From the late 1950s, Henri Tajfel and his students, first at Oxford University and then later at Bristol University, explored the consequences of categorization.[13] Their research suggests that when some objects or people are placed in "group X" and other objects or people are placed in "group Y," two consequences arise for those looking at groups X and Y. First, the differences between group X and group Y tend to be exaggerated. Thus, for example, we are likely to end up with gross stereotypes and simplifications, such as "Men are from Mars, Women are from Venus," arguing that there are enormous psychological differences between men and women. Such exaggerations neglect the empirical evidence showing that in all major psychological characteristics, men and women are actually very similar. A second consequence of categorization is that differences within groups are minimized; thus all those in group X are seen as more similar than they really are, just as the members of group Y are seen as more similar than they really are (leading to such exaggerations as, "men hate shopping" and "women love to shop").

Evolutionary psychologists, another important group of researchers who focus on inbuilt characteristics, have gained enormous influence since the 1970s, particularly through the ideas of E.O. Wilson in the United States and Richard Dawkins in England.[14] Dawkins is the author of *The Selfish Gene*[15] and probably the most revolutionary evolutionary theorist since Charles Darwin. The new evolutionary thesis shifts the focus to the genetic level and to competition for survival between gene pools. The function of humans, it is proposed, is to serve as convenient vehicles for the survival of genes. The thoughts and action of humans are structured by a "whispering within," the silent influence of genes. For example, people tend to be more cooperative with others who are genetically more similar to themselves, and to show aggression against genetically dissimilar others. The same genetic factors are assumed to lead to gender differences, so that, for example, females are likely to be more conservative about their choice of mates (because they can have fewer children and invest more highly in each child, females try to ensure that the investments they make are with the most fit partner possible) and males are likely to fall in and out of love more easily (because they are genetically programmed to try to spread their genes through sheer numbers—even if they are "heels," it is because of their genes).

Thus, evolutionary psychologists depict the psychological citizen as driven to act in favor of the genetic in-group and against the genetic out-group. According to this viewpoint, political life is only superficially about ideologies, and political parties rallying around competing ideologies, such as "conservative" vs. "liberal." At a deeper level such "surface" ideological differences reflect genetic differences.

The vision of the psychological citizen that is put forward by schools of psychologists in the first category places stress on inbuilt characteristics, and certain universals assumed to be common to all humankind. We are not concerned with the details of how the different schools emphasize different features of assumed "universals," but one topic I want to highlight is the link between categorization and identity. A general assumption in the research literature, formalized in the 1970s through *social identity theory*,[16] is that all humans are motivated to achieve a positive and distinct social identity. Simply put, it is proposed that humans are motivated to belong to groups that are evaluated positively and seen as having distinct characteristics. This important idea highlights "fixed," universal identity needs and suggests limits to how much identity can be manipulated. We return to this crucial issue of identity needs in later chapters.

Group Two: The "Constructed" Nature of the Psychological Citizen

How malleable is the psychological citizen? How much can we change the characteristics of this creature? The first group of schools we considered highlights characteristics assumed to be fixed and integral to the "nature" of the psychological citizen, whereas the second group assumes that this creature is malleable and can be reshaped into just about any form.

Any discussion of the plasticity of human beings has to begin with the sensational "behaviorist manifesto" propagated by John Watson (1878–1958) in 1913, which dismissed all references to human consciousness and gave center stage to the prediction and control of overt, objectively verifiable behavior. The behaviorists[17] took their starting point to be John Locke's (1632–1704) metaphor for the mind as *tabula rasa* (blank slate); life experiences would make marks on this blank slate, and through experience the story of a life would be written. The direction and end result of this story would depend entirely on the circumstances a person experienced. The behaviorist claim was that through properly designed reinforcement schedules, it was possible to shape a young child into just about any kind of adult, to become a plumber, a nurse, a journalist, a politician, or whatever else we design for.

The political and ethical implications of behaviorism for the psychological citizen were developed most fully by B.F. Skinner (1904–1990), and perhaps because of this Skinner became the most controversial and famous of all behaviorists. Early in his career, in his novel *Walden II* that was published just after the World War II, Skinner presented a fictional account of a human world that was socially engineered on the basis of behaviorist principles.

In the original work entitled *Walden*, the American transcendentalist writer Henry Thoreau (1817–1862) had described his experiences of living in isolation in the woods surrounding Walden Pond. Thoreau's return to nature was intended as a journey of discovery about the essentials of life,

I went to the woods because I wished to live deliberately, to front only the essential facts of life, and see if I could not learn what it had to teach, and not, when I came to die, discover that I had not lived. I did not wish to live what was not life.... [18]

Thoreau's assumption was that living "in nature," he would be free to discover what life really is. Nevertheless, for Skinner, such freedom is an illusion. All organisms, including humans, are shaped by their environments. Even something as "uncontrolled" and "natural" as emotions is actually shaped through reinforcements, as explained by Frazier, the protagonist of Skinner's *Walden Two* who in the passage below is answering questions from a sceptic:

"How do you make sure that jealousy isn't needed in *Walden Two*?" I said.

"In *Walden Two* problems can't be solved by attacking others," said Frazier with marked finality.

"That's not the same as eliminating jealousy, though," I said.

"Of course it's not. But when a particular emotion is no longer a useful part of the behavioral repertoire, we proceed to eliminate it."

"Yes, but how?"

"It's simply a matter of behavioral engineering." [19]

In this sense, no human can be "free," because all environments, including the woods, control our behavior through environmental reinforcers. We should move beyond the question of whether or not behavior should be controlled, because it *is* controlled, to the question of toward what ends we should shape behavior through environmental engineering.

Of course, the idea that human thought and action is shaped by the environment runs against our ideas of human dignity. We prefer to think of ourselves as deciding our own fate and being able to live freely, in any way that we choose to do so. But Skinner believes this perspective is archaic. In another controversial work, *Beyond Freedom and Dignity*,[20] Skinner argues that instead of remaining loyal to such outdated notions of human freedom and dignity, and denying the power of the environment to shape our behavior, we should focus our energies on better designing the environments that shape us.

Although Skinner's views have been attacked as regressive and going against basic democratic principles, some of his main concerns are very much in line with twenty-first- century thinking, for example as reflected in his discussion of environmental pollution. Of course, in fighting pollution, his strategy is to rely on "the science of behavioral engineering" rather than moral "sermons" about how each person should consume less. Back in 1976 he wrote, "To induce people to adapt to new ways of living which are less consuming and hence less polluting, we do not need to speak of frugality or austerity as if we meant sacrifice. There are contingencies of reinforcement in which people continue to pursue (and even overtake) happiness while consuming far less than they now consume. The experimental analysis of behavior has clearly shown that it is not the quantity of goods that count (as the law of supply and demand suggests) but the contingent relation between goods and behavior."[21] What and how we consume, Skinner argues, can be reshaped because it depends on reinforcement schedules integral to the context, rather than fixed characteristics internal to us.

Social Constructionism and "Human Nature"

The second group of thinkers who emphasize the plasticity of the psychological citizen are the social constructionists, who have been particularly influential since the 1980s.[22] In contrast to radical behaviorists who reject any reference to subjective experience and cognition, the social constructionists focus on how individuals and groups subjectively interpret the world and create social realities. Whereas the behaviorists focus on how behavior is shaped by the environment and reject a role for human intentionality, social constructionists propose that social reality is intentionally constructed by humans collectively, and adopted by individuals through participation in collective life. Instead of a focus on "stimuli" in the environment as in the behaviorist tradition, social constructionists explore the stories people tell about themselves and their world. Narratives about our own lives and the lives of others help to uphold and propagate particular versions of social reality. There is considerable flexibility in the social reality we agree upon and collectively uphold.

As an example of the plasticity of human behavior, social constructionists point to the enormous variations found in the kind of gender relationships considered "correct" across different cultures. Should women have the right to drive cars and participate in political life? What seems like a natural and "inalienable" right in some contexts is not accepted as such in many other contexts. In 2008 it is considered a major "breakthrough" for citizens in Saudi Arabia to raise the question of whether women should be permitted to drive automobiles; at this rate, it will be a long time before Saudi women play a serious role in political leadership—contrast this with the situation in India, Sri Lanka, and Pakistan, countries where women have been the head of state. They not only drive their own cars, they are at the wheel at the head of the nation.[23]

"We can arrange gender relations to take any shape we want!" This is the message of social constructionism. We can give women no role in politics and no rights in the public sphere, not even the right to drive a car, or we can give women a full role in politics and make them national political leaders. There is no "natural" path here, just the path we choose to take. But once a path is chosen, then those who participate will come to see the path as "natural."

To drive this point home, consider the way families are organized across different cultures. What could be more natural than a husband and wife as the basis of the family? But in some cultural traditions, *polygamy* is "natural," where a man has more than one wife. For example, polygamy is still practised among some groups of Mormons in the United States (although it is prohibited by federal law). In addition, in Islamic countries all Muslim men are allowed up to four wives at any one time. On the other hand, there are also societies that practice *polyandry*, the marriage of one woman with more than one husband. Indeed, there are varieties of polyandry, such as the case of the Nyinba of Nepal who practice *fraternal polyandry*, where all brothers in a family marry the same woman.

In all of these different variations of male–female relations in marriage, the participants describe their own arrangement as "natural" and "correct." For example, whereas westerners typically find the idea of fraternal polyandry grotesque, the anthropologist Melvyn Goldstein points out that, "The eldest brother is normally dominant in terms of authority, that is, in managing the household, but all the brothers share the work and participate as sexual partners. Tibetan males and females do not find the sexual aspect of sharing a spouse the least bit unusual, repulsive, or scandalous, and the norm is for the wife to treat all the brothers the same."[24] Western researchers typically explain fraternal polyandry in terms of its usefulness in controlling the population and sharing resources,[25] but the natives involved describe it as the "natural" way for husbands and wife to live.

CONCLUDING COMMENT

In this chapter we have seen that there is enormous variation as to the degree to which researchers believe human behavior is malleable. Whereas one group of researchers, such as the sociobiologists and cognitive psychologists, highlight the inbuilt, "hard-wired," fixed features of human characteristics, a second group, such as the behaviorists and the social constructionists, depict humans as malleable and flexible, capable of being reengineered or reconstructed by environmental circumstances.

I have identified a third path, using the distinction between performance capacity and performance style as the point of departure.

Certain human characteristics, those that fall under the umbrella of performance capacity, are hardwired and not changed by changing circumstances. For example, if Joe has a motorcycle accident, hits his head against a lamppost, and experiences a loss of auditory capacity, this becomes part of the "fixed" characteristics of Joe. The brain injury Joe unfortunately suffered impacts his hearing in a way that falls under the umbrella of performance capacity. The meaning that Joe ascribed to his accident ("It was an act of God," "It was bad luck," "It was my fate," and so on), on the other hand, concerns performance style. Performance style can be changed through changes in context, at least to some degree.

The question I turn to next is, to what extent is it possible to change behaviors that fall under the umbrella of performance style? Are there any limits to how changing contexts can change performance style behaviors? I argue that there are such limits, and that these limits reflect certain universals in human social behavior, the most basic being collective identity needs that enhance survival chances. Under certain conditions, when a group perceives the possibility of in-group demise and extinction, threats to such universal needs result in violent backlash.

CHAPTER 3

Universal Needs and the Psychological Roots of Radicalization and Terrorism

"Darn those Muslim fanatics!"

The middle-aged, grossly overweight man in front of me was having a hard time reaching down to take off his shoes. We were in a very long, tedious line of forlorn looking people, passing through the security section of Ronald Reagan National Airport in Washington, DC.

"You know, every time I pass through one of these damned security places, I get madder at Osama bin Laden and them Muslim fanatics," he grumbled as he finally managed to get his shoes off and put them on the tray to pass through the security system.

"String up all the fanatics," added his companion, a taller and even plumper man who had sat on the floor to sort out his belongings and was having difficulties getting up on his feet again, "but don't forget the nuts on our side who got us into the Iraq war. Let's not forget our fanatics."

"There you go again, you liberals just don't understand. There's gonna be war. Do you wanna fight it over there or over here?"

"True enough, as long as fanatics are so active on both sides, as long as the nuts are leading us, there'll be war."

"You really don't know human nature."

"That's one thing we agree on, it's about human nature."

We finally got through the security screening and the two men disappeared in the airport crowds, still debating as they waddled and bumped their way through the throngs.

Their debate raised questions in my mind about human nature, and what, if anything, we humans have in common. Can we better understand ourselves by returning to the question of human nature, and digging deeper into our common characteristics?

Using the terminology I introduced earlier, it is fairly straightforward to identify shared human characteristics in the domain of performance capacity, in how well we are able to carry out actions. Most humans irrespective of ethnicity, race, gender, and other group memberships, are very similar in how well they see, hear, remember, and so on.

However, what about the domain of performance style, how we carry out actions, and the meanings we give to what we do? Is it the case that our social meaning systems and the social needs that we have are completely dependent on local cultures, and vary from one society to another? Or, are there certain aspects of the social meaning systems and social needs that are common to all human cultures?

The main argument of this chapter is that although there are what the biologist Paul Ehrlich calls "human natures,"[1] there are also a limited number of universal psychological needs that people are strongly motivated to satisfy.

PRIMITIVES: PSYCHOLOGICAL UNIVERSALS

Universals in social behavior are shaped by a combination of common human characteristics, both biological and environmental. These give rise to common features of human cultures, features that are essential for the survival of human societies and that are passed on from generation to generation. Of course, there are enormous variations across cultures as to how cultures are passed on. For example, there are differences in the carriers used in different cultures to pass on values and beliefs (in Chapter 1, the illustrative examples of the Islamic veil and the U.S. national flag were used to discuss the concept of carrier).

In this discussion I want to focus particularly on a category of universals that I call *primitives*,[2] environmentally shaped behaviors that are universal, functional, and absolutely essential for the survival of humans both as individuals and groups. I will first illustrate the nature of primitives by discussing the example of *turn-taking in communications*: in all human societies, and also some animal groups individuals in interaction must take turns in order for effective communications to take place. Having familiarized ourselves with the concept of primitives, I will then discuss the characteristics of four primitives that play a vital role in the context of the Near and Middle East, these being

(1) *The Psychological Social Contract*: The psychological processes involved in the integration of individuals in the larger sociopolitical order, so that the individual successfully enters into society and the larger culture enters into the individual.

(2) *Trust*: The minimal level of interpersonal and intergroup trust that has to be present in order for a society to function effectively and survive.

(3) *Psychological Control*: The minimal level of perceived control that individuals need to feel they have over their collective and individual lives, in order to feel secure and autonomous.

(4) *Identity Needs*: The fundamental need for positive and distinct identity that has to be satisfied in order for individuals to serve as constructive group members.

I shall begin, then, by explaining the concept of primitives more fully through the example of turn taking in communications.

Turn-Taking in Communications

I first became sensitive to the importance of turn-taking in communications when I found myself, either as a researcher or a tourist, in societies where I did not speak the local language. In order to communicate using nonverbal signals and a few words learned from a dictionary of the local language or from local people, it is essential that turn-taking takes place. Of course, turn-taking is also essential when we communicate in our own heritage languages. Just think about what happens when a group of people are talking with one another and they fail to take turns: communications break down very quickly.

One of the essential skills we teach children is to take turns in speaking. A common and constant refrain from parents in training their children is, "Don't interrupt! Wait for your turn to speak." Children gradually learn the intricate skill of joining in conversations by inserting their verbal contributions at the correct times. This means acquiring the ability to correctly interpret the various verbal and nonverbal cues available in the situation to indicate when it would be appropriate for the child to enter the dialogue. "Not now, wait your turn," is a familiar response to the child, as she or he goes through numerous trial and error efforts to learn turn-taking in communications.

The basic building-block of interpersonal turn-taking, which probably has its roots in activity cycles associated with mother–infant feeding interactions, leads into a variety of turn-taking activities at the collective level. For example, turn-taking plays an essential role as the "grease" that allows the flow of traffic in modern cities, as cars take turns at traffic intersections. Even when there are no traffic lights or police officers to regulate turn-taking, drivers in most instances take turns routinely and correctly. Turn-taking also plays important roles in the law and politics: lawyers in court cases take turns in cross examining witnesses, and term-limits guarantee that the holders of political office must step aside in order that others will "have a turn" in positions of political power. Through these examples we see how the basic building block of turn-taking evolves as integral to complex collective practices within a cultural system.

In the context of the Near and Middle East, turn-taking in politics has evolved along a path that is far from democratic. Instead of "term limits," political leaders who attain positions of power use their influence to try to achieve and extend a power monopoly for as long as possible. Thus, there are in Egypt, Syria, Iran, Saudi Arabia, and various other countries in the region leaders who remain in power for the duration of their lives, using a variety of titles such as "president," "king," "supreme spiritual leader," and so on. Of course, in all these cases the (obviously false) pretext is that the leader has remained in power because of the support and the good will of the people. The truth is that in these societies, once a "supreme leader" comes to power, the only means the people have to get him out of power is to kill him or to launch a successful bloody revolution.

I now turn to consider four other primitives that are particularly important in the context of the Near and Middle East, starting with the psychological social contract that serves to bind individuals to societies.

The Psychological Social Contract

"No man is an island, entire of itself; every man is a piece of the continent, a part of the main."

—John Donne[3]

""It was I—" began Raskolnikov

"Have some hot water."

Raskolnikov pushed the glass of water away and said softly but distinctly, pausing after each word:

"It was I who killed the old woman money-lender and her sister Lisaveta with a hatchet and robbed them.""

—Dostoyevsky[4]

Raskolnikov, the protagonist in Fyodor Dostoyevsky's (1821–1881) novel *Crime and Punishment*, is an illustration of John Donne's (1572–1631) proclamation that no person "is an island, entire of itself." The secret of his terrible crime, the murders he has committed for the sake of money, has cut Raskolnikov away from the rest of humanity. However, his isolation proves unbearable, and in the end he admits to his crime and reconnects with the rest of society. Human beings are linked to the social group because of practical needs, but in a more profound way we are connected to the collectivity through a vital need for psychological bonds. It was in order to restore such psychological bonds that Raskolnikov confessed his bloody crimes.

The need for a bond with the social group, as reflected in the case of Raskolnikov, arose through cultural evolution, as individuals with stronger bonds with their social groups survived and taught their skills to the next generation. Individuals with weaker bonds to their social groups did not benefit from the protection and support provided by groups, and lived riskier lives. There was a gradual shift in human cultures toward groups that give higher value to what in modern terms is summed up as "team spirit"—being motivated to work for the success of the group, being concerned to achieve a positive group identity, standing up for one's group, and so on.

Of course, an important aspect of the human experience is also individuality and "standing apart" from the group.[5] Individuals do not like to be completely absorbed and "lost" in the collectivity. From a functional perspective, individuality and being different is a valuable source of innovation and change in the way things are done. Consequently, there is a continued tension between the need to belong and conform to group norms, and the need to stand apart and to "be different." There is some cross-cultural variation on these themes. For example, on the surface "being different" and "standing out" are more valued in the United States than in Japan. However, we need to look at such surface differences skeptically. The American television advertisement tells us to "dare to be different and buy brand X jeans," and we might even "feel different" when we wear brand X jeans, but the fact is that the same advertisement sold brand X jeans to 10 million other Americans, who now all "feel different." The research suggests that conformity and "standing out" in America is about the same as in other major societies.[6] This is not surprising, given the evolutionary developed need to belong, shared by all human groups.

As the Greek philosophers famously pointed out over 2,500 years ago, human beings are social animals, our natural inclination being to live in groups. But in joining groups, we are forced to give up part of our individual autonomy and freedoms. There is a continuous tension between the demands of the individual for personal freedom, autonomy, and independence, and the restrictions and demands placed on the individual by the larger society. Thomas Hobbes[7] (1588–1679), John Locke[8] (1631–1704), David Hume[9] (1711–1776), and Jean Jacques Rousseau[10] (1712–1778) are among the modern philosophers who have discussed the resolution of this tension under the topic "social contract" (Rousseau is actually the originator of the term social contract, *du contrat social*). I have termed the "classic" concept of the social contract, as per discussions of Roussea and others,[11] the "logical social contract," because the working assumption is that sometime in the historical past the rulers and the ruled had actually worked out and agreed upon a contract to regulate relations between them.

Discussions of the "logical social contract" have not been concerned with the historical or anthropological accuracy of the assumption that a contract had been agreed upon in the past. A contract must have been agreed upon, because in those early days of living in woods and deserts under natural conditions, given that humans are of fairly equal physical and mental abilities, it would have been impossible for one person or a small group to impose their will on the majority of people scattered around different geographical areas. The logical social contract was a fairly "democratic" idea, because it assumed that government has originally evolved through the consent of the people, and presumably if people became unhappy with their governments they could change their minds and annul the social contract that their ancestors had agreed upon.

The revolutionary feature of the social contract was that it placed obligations on the rulers as well as the ruled. In this way, it build on the idea of reciprocal rights and duties between the rulers and the ruled already inherent in the *Magna Carta*, an agreement signed by King John of England in 1215. But the "black-letter law" that is represented by the Magna Carta, Declaration of Human Rights, and other formal documents come much later than the informal rules of rights and duties that have regulated human behavior for at least tens of thousands of years.[12]

Trust

It might seem paradoxical that I am proposing trust as a basic psychological necessity for the survival of a society, given that the twenty-first century is often regarded as an age of distrust. Everywhere we turn, the signs seem to be unambiguous, declaring distrust rather than trust to be the norm.

Consider, for example, trust in politicians and the political system. In the sole superpower of our twenty-first- century world, participation in even the most important political elections is down to about 50 percent of the eligible electorate, and people generally seem to have low regard and low trust for politicians and the *status quo* in politics (and thus the tremendous enthusiasm for the theme of "change" in the 2008 U.S. Presidential elections).

The focus on distrust is probably in part a result of the increased mobility of populations and the decline of traditional community and group allegiances. As documented by a variety of social scientists, increasing industrialization and integration within the global economy leads to a decline in ties based on traditional family, ethnic, tribal, and local allegiances. At the extreme, this is represented by trends in the United States, where individualism and "going it alone" are highest, and where membership in community and group activities, from Boy Scouts and Girl Guides to community networks, have been declining. On the surface, at least, these trends seem to suggest that people are placing trust in themselves, and investing in the future of the self rather than the community. In this sense, at least, the "self help" aspect of the American conservative movement is going against the "community building" aspect of the same movement.

Distrust is also associated with an anti-foreigner sentiment prevalent in the United States and western Europe. The enormous numbers of illegal immigrants in the West, estimated at about 10–14 million in the United States and about 6–8 million in Europe (in 2008), together with enormous societal transformations and economic changes, have helped fuel an anti-foreigner atmosphere. "Don't trust the outsiders!" That seems to be the message of nationalist-oriented media channels.

The so-called "war on terror" has added further to the atmosphere of distrust, particularly in the United States. On the one hand the general population is constantly bombarded with information about "terror alerts" and potential or actual "terror attacks," and the need for everyone to be vigilant and to report "suspicious activity" to the authorities. On the other hand, the federal government has itself become the object of distrust because government agencies are now known to have engaged in a variety of illegal activities, from wiretapping to kidnaping of supposed "terror suspects," some of whom have turned out to be innocent.

Of course, distrust of the U.S. Federal government increased in the first decade of the twenty-first century because of what proved to be false information used by the George W. Bush administration to justify the invasion of Iraq in 2003. The original justification for the invasion, the presence of weapons of mass destruction in Iraq, proved to be false, and an equally false justification, the "support of Iraq for the terrorist group al-Qaeda," was fabricated as a replacement. Not surprisingly, being tricked into supporting a war that at the time of the publication of this book has cost close to three trillion dollars, when basic child health care and educational programs remain unfunded in the United States, gradually led to a rise in distrust among the American population.

Given this general atmosphere of distrust, both among the population within the United States and among populations around the world toward the U.S. government, am I justified in claiming that trust is a "primitive" social relation that is essential for the functioning and survival of society? Am I justified in claiming that trust is a generic societal norm? I believe I am, and my position is shown to be correct when we consider the norms of everyday life in societies around the world.

All societies survive using a norm of trust, meaning that most people most of the time behave as if they trust one another. For example, imagine you are visiting Washington, DC, and you get lost and need to find your way to the National Gallery of Art. You stop and ask a passerby the best way to get to the National Gallery, and he tells you the best way is to go by Metro rail. You find the Metro station and ask another stranger which platform to stand on and when the next train is expected. When you finally arrive at the National Gallery of Art, there are long lines for the exhibit you want to see, but a guard tells you to come back after lunch and the lines will have disappeared. You take his advice and go for lunch, planning to return after lunch. Consider this sequence of everyday events: they are extraordinary in the sense that at every step you have shown trust. You trusted complete strangers to tell you the truth when you asked the way to the National Gallery, to the correct platform in the train station, and so on. In our everyday lives, we routinely put our trust in other people, sometimes complete strangers.

Of course, there are some individuals we learn to distrust, and some situations in which we have less trust. For example, if a person is shown by experience to be a habitual liar, or if a situation is dangerous (as when we are ourselves strangers passing through a drug-infested, high-crime neighborhood), we will become distrustful. However, for most people, these are the exceptions rather than the rule.

In the societies of the Near and Middle East, trust is high among family members, but distrust has become the norm in relationships with local officials, governments, and western powers. Distrust toward the United States is particularly high. Muslims around the world feel that the West holds negative views toward them.[13] Muslims want to be respected and trusted, but at the same time they tend not to trust the U.S. government.

Perceived Lack of Control

Pierre: " ... in the universe, in the whole universe, there is a kingdom of truth, and we who are now the children of earth are—in the eternal sense—children of the whole universe. Don't I feel in my soul that I am a part of that vast, harmonious whole? ... I feel not only that I cannot vanish, since nothing in this world ever vanishes, but that I always shall exist and always have existed ... "

"Yes ... ," commented Prince Andrei, "but that won't convince me, my dear boy—life and death are what convince ... "

—Tolstoy[14]

This exchange between Pierre and Prince Andrei, central characters in Leo Tolstoy's universal novel *War and Peace*, takes place at a time when both men have had traumatic experiences that ruptured their relationships with the larger society and forced them to try to reposition themselves. Pierre and Prince Andrei both feel that they have lost control of their lives, that they are being controlled by circumstances and by others. This perception of having too little control arises out of real crises in their relationships, and in the direction of their lives. Pierre has become separated from his wife, after fighting a duel and seriously wounding the man who he believed was having an affair with her. Prince Andrei has been injured in the Napoleonic wars and returned home just in time to witness his wife die after giving birth to their son.

In searching for ways to deal with their different tragedies and their feelings of having lost control over the direction of their lives, the two men temporarily settle on divergent paths: Pierre takes a path that positions him as both merged within and at one with the rest of the universe, whereas Prince Andrei stands aloof and is awed by the abyss of death. For both men, how they are positioned at this point proves to be temporary, and the stream of life carries them along to other positions, beyond their personal tragedies. Gradually, they come to feel once again that they have regained adequate control over the course of their lives, even though these experiences are in large part based on illusions of control.

The experience of Pierre and Prince Andrei leads us to reflect back on the broad question of the human need for control.[15] There are two aspects to this need. On the one hand, there is a functional advantage for individuals to have a minimal level of control in their lives: some control over their environments, their social relationships, their rights and responsibilities, and so on. Out of this functional advantage arose a need for control, and a pleasure in having control. One of the ways in which we punish people is to deprive them of control in important domains; for example, we place convicted criminals in jail, where prisoners have little control. A second aspect of the need for control is that the experience of control is subjective and associated with emotions: the threat of having too little control can be associated with fear and anxiety. Globalization is leading to these experiences, as the world seems to be becoming a place where individuals have less and less control over events that take place in distant lands but nevertheless impact on their personal lives and local communities.

Whereas a few centuries ago, the vast majority of people knew only the local village or city neighborhood, now economic forces are pushing the local into the background and placing larger and larger groups into the foreground. In the age of globalization, psychological citizens around the world are being asked to enter into, identify with, and incorporate the values of larger and larger social groups. How feasible is this change? Can the psychological citizen transform to meet this demand?

Globalization forces have heightened the uncontrollable impact of events in other parts of the world, events that seem remote but are nevertheless changing our daily experiences. This is not limited to just economic events (that raise the price of goods and the expenses of day-to-day activities, make whole sets of jobs at home disappear, and wipe out entire industries overnight), but also political, religious, and cultural events. Suddenly, a cartoon published in Denmark can ignite an explosion of protest on the other side of the world among Muslims who see the cartoon as insulting to them and their religion, resulting in a backlash that floods back into Denmark and all of western Europe, and threatens to drown the cartoonist and the newspaper in which the cartoon dared to first appear. Even seemingly small events, such as the publication of a cartoon, are no longer just to be considered in their local and national contexts, because they can have global reach, reactions, and repercussions. This trend has important new implications for our sense of control.

My contention is that the psychological citizen has come under new types of distress, and in some societies the distress associated with globalization is leading to radicalization, conflict, extreme violence, and terrorism. One set of reasons has to do with basic psychological needs, and the stress placed on the relationship between both in-groups and out-groups (a point I discuss further below). A second set of reasons has to do with perceptions of declining control, and a sense that we have little or no control over important events in our lives. Globalizations means that even national governments seem to be losing control over the course of events within national borders.

While the need for control is universal, so that all humans need to feel they have a minimal level of control over their lives, the feeling that globalization and macro political–economic trends are out of one's control is particularly high in the Muslim societies of the Near and Middle East. On the one hand, the enormous energy and other natural resources of the region provide fantastic opportunities for the people of the region to experience economic and cultural growth. On the other hand, the corrupt and inefficient governments of the region provide no hope for real improvements in the life conditions of the masses.

Identity Needs

I have already discussed some key aspects of identity needs earlier in this book. In an earlier book, *From the Terrorists' Point of View* (2006), I argued that a widespread identity crisis in Islamic communities underlies the present radicalization being experienced by these communities, as well as the terrorism emanating from them. In discussions around the theme of the so-called "war on terror," identity has not been given adequate attention. Identity is often depicted as a "soft" rather than "hard" issue, to do with how people think about themselves and the world around them, rather than about "hard" material things like bombs and guns. I am returning now to further explore the nature of identity needs, and the relationship between globalization and identity threat, because the topic is on the one hand of the greatest importance, and on the other hand utterly neglected in discussions about radicalization and terrorism, although more recently some have payed it lip service.

We must accept identity needs as a basic universal primitive, because in human evolutionary processes identity plays a central role in the functioning and successful survival of groups. Far from being something "soft" and a side effect of "hard" material factors, identity has been central and essential to everything humans do to survive in groups and as individuals. The role played by identity in group survival can be best understood by first considering mechanisms of control and cohesion in group life.

Throughout our evolutionary history, we humans have survived through successfully organizing ourselves into groups and living as members of communities. For the most part we lived in mobile groups, as hunter-gatherers, but in the last twenty thousand years or so we gradually developed settlements and abandoned the nomadic life, although hundreds of groups of nomads still continue their migrations each year in different parts of the world. A continuous challenge throughout this evolutionary processes has been how to manage different individuals into a cohesive group, how to prevent the needs and motivations of individuals from breaking up the group (earlier in this chapter we discussed the idea of a "social contract," assumed to have evolved to help bind individuals to the larger community). A group would be more successful if individual members found room to show innovation and discover new ways of doing things, but at the same time felt bound to the group enough to cooperate in achieving group goals. The successful group provides room for individual talents to flourish, but is organized to harness the fruits of individual talents to achieve collective goals.

Identity is integral to the psychological social contract, it is the glue that binds individuals to the group, but at the same time allows some measure of individual autonomy and differentness. Group members are socialized into group identity step by step, and it is through group identity that individuals come to a acquire a sense of belonging to the group. This sense of belonging and allegiance to the group evolves slowly as the individual takes on group carriers, such as flags, mascots, slogans, mottos, anthems, and the like. Carriers can become sacred and also include parts of the physical environment, such as "sacred mountains" and buildings.

A vitally important carrier is the leader, not just the personality of the leader but the leadership position or the official "office" of the leader. For example, in the United States, a distinction is made in practice between the Office of the U.S. President and the person who occupies this office. Through this distinction, respect for the office of the president can be maintained and continuity can be achieved in the organization of the group, even when the person holding that office comes to be disliked or perhaps disdained. Thus, a leader can be expelled from office, but the office can continue to be respected, as the old chant goes, "The King is dead, long live the King." The leader can help direct the energies of the group members to achieve group goals and maintain group cohesion in the face of external threats.

Through making group identity salient, the behavior of group members can be influenced. Group identity brings into effect group norms and leads to conformity to group norms and obedience to group leaders. Thus, for example, by invoking "American identity," "pride in country," and so on, Americans can be influenced to show patriotic behavior, such as support for war, including enlisting in the military to fight for "one's country" and making the ultimate sacrifice. Because group identity is so powerful in shaping the behavior of group members, there is a constant struggle between power factions within a group to define group identity. For example, in the United States there are contests between political factions to define what it is to be "a patriot." Do real patriots question and criticize the president's actions in order to avoid war whenever possible and to launch a more effective campaign when war is unavoidable, or do real patriots obey the president unquestioningly in order to present a united front against the enemy?

Separate from group identity, each individual has a distinct personal identity. The vast bulk of research has focused on identity at the individual level, because this research has been conducted by scholars from highly individualistic cultures, such as the United States. However, individual identity takes shape within the context of collective identity, and it is collective identity to which I give priority in this discussion—particularly when considering the role of identity in Islamic communities.

In order to better understand the experiences of collective or group identity in Islamic communities, it is useful to also introduce the concept of *relative deprivation*, how deprived or well-off a person feels relative to comparison targets (such as other groups of people). Feelings of deprivation are subjective and are influenced by whom we select as our comparison targets. For example, I am writing this section of this chapter during a visit to the Grand Bahamas, and I can make myself feel very deprived by comparing my financial situation to that of the international rich who have second homes in the Bahamas and enjoy their lives on enormous yachts, private jet planes, and luxurious oceanfront villas, or I can make myself feel highly privileged by comparing my situation to that of the poorest Bahamians who live in poverty-stricken neighborhoods and suffer poor health and educational services.

Relative Deprivation in Islamic Communities

In his seminal study on relative deprivation, Runciman[16] distinguished between *egoistical relative deprivation*, when an individual feels personally deprived as a result of making interpersonal comparisons between himself and others (for example, how deprived I feel when I compare my personal situation with that of particular other Bahamnians), and *fraternal relative deprivation*, when group members feel deprived because of the situation of their group relative to other groups (for example, when I compare the situation of university professors with certain groups of Bahamians, such as yacht owners or shack dwellers). The relative salience of egoistical and fraternal relative deprivation is dependent on culture and contextual factors. In the context of Islamic communities, fraternal relative deprivation is highly prominent, because people are encouraged to compare their group situation with that of out-groups.

Muslim communities, and particularly Muslim fundamentalists, are experiencing fraternal relative deprivation. In domains such as "democracy" and "human rights," Muslim fundamentalists perceive themselves to be the target of unfair attacks by the West and particularly the United States. On the one hand, Muslim fundamentalists see western democracy as incompatible with Islam, particularly on issues such as the rights of women. On the other hand, even when Muslims attempt to put democracy into practice, they hit a brick wall, because American practice and rhetoric are contradictory. In practice, the United States supports "pro American" dictatorships in the Near and Middle East, but in rhetoric American politicians and media ask, "Why will Muslims not accept democracy?"

Muslims see American support for democracy in the Near and Middle East as disingenuous, and this has added to Muslim feelings of fraternal deprivation. From the 1953 CIA-engineered coup that toppled the democratically elected Prime Minister (Mohammed Mossadegh, 1881–1967) and reinstated the dictatorship of the Shah in Iran, to the spoiling of the outcomes of democratic elections in Palestine, experience has proven that the United States will only accept the outcomes of democratic elections if they result in pro-American groups coming to power but not if anti-American groups such as Hamas win elections and acquire power. When elections lead to outcomes not seen to be in the interests of the United States, then American influence is used to spoil that outcome. In practice, the United States wages unjust wars, such as the war in Iraq that, since 2003, has resulted directly or indirectly in the deaths of well over half a million Iraqis and created millions of Iraqi refugees, but in rhetoric American politicians and media "support human rights." These contradictions also have repercussions for the American culture and frame of mind, an issue further explored in Chapter 9.

Threatened Needs

I have argued that there are certain basic universals in behavior, termed primitive social relations, without which human survival is seriously threatened. All primitive social relations are essential to survival, but in the context of Islamic communities in the twenty-first century, the importance and centrality of identity needs has increased. This is in large part because fractured globalization results in far greater contact with strangers and out-groups, either directly or through the media. Such contact highlights the question: What kind of a person am I? What kind of groups do I belong to? What is our future in this fast-changing world? From the perspective of traditional and fundamentalist Muslims, globalization involves westernization (and particularly Americanization), associated with the influx of western values, norms, and identity ideals. These changes are perceived as moving Muslim communities, and particularly the young in these communities, in the wrong direction.

Of course, not all Muslims perceive globalization as a threat, and indeed some, such as Muslim women seeking greater freedom and equality, see globalization as creating favorable opportunities for change. But traditionalists and fundamentalists have used every opportunity to interpret globalization changes as a threat to the survival of Muslim societies. What happens when group identity and other primitive social relations are perceived to be threatened? I turn to this question next.

GROUP DEFENSE MECHANISMS

Through evolutionary processes, all life forms have developed defense mechanisms that are designed to increase their survival chances. Of course, defense mechanisms function with different levels of success, and some prove not to be effective enough, resulting in the extinction of a life form.

Defense mechanisms function at all levels, from the micro cellular and molecular level related to protection from diseases, to the macro level of defense mechanisms adopted by societies to protect cultural systems (including cultural values, ideologies, beliefs, norms, and so on). At the micro level, we have made tremendous advances in the field of immunology and in understanding the biological and biochemical aspects of the immune system that protects us from disease.[17] We are also making progress in better understanding how the natural environment is reacting to environmental pollution, such as the defense mechanisms triggered in plants by pollution.[18] Research on animals has also revealed a wide variety of defense mechanisms developed by potential prey to avoid being eaten by predators, common ones being camouflage, mimicking an animal that is dangerous to the predator, ejecting chemicals poisonous to the predator, or simply using speed to escape the predator.

In the human world, also, defense mechanisms are used in a variety of ways. For example, organizations continually upgrade the defenses of their computer systems against attacks by outsiders.[19] "Anti-virus" programs are now a part of the daily lives of all computer users. Also, in the business marketplace, organizations are continually on the guard against "hostile takeovers" by rival companies, using various maneuvers to get themselves in advantageous positions so as to avoid unwanted takeovers. Defense mechanisms are also triggered when cultural groups feel threatened, and particularly when group members perceive their way of life could end.

In Chapter 6, I further explore radicalization and terrorism as one form of "defense mechanism" adopted by human groups that perceive a high level of external threat and possible extinction. For now, it is useful to highlight the irrational nature of most collective human defense mechanisms, meaning that we are not consciously aware of why we are adopting, or even that we are adopting, a particular behavioral strategy. Human beings are brilliant at rationalizing their actions after the fact, so that there is seldom a lack of articulated reason for violence—whether the violence involves an individual carrying out a terrorist attack or a nation invading another nation. Even the most destructive acts of terrorism and war are rationalized by reference to higher ideals ("justice," "democracy," "defense of our faith," "freedom," and so on), and this rationalization is itself integral to the defense mechanism adopted.

CONCLUDING COMMENT

The collective behavior of human groups is the outcome of numerous complex historical, psychological, economic, and cultural factors in interaction, leading to outcomes that are in some important respects unique. Consider, for example, the artistic flowering that took place in Renaissance Italy, or the revolutionary ideas that emerged in late eighteenth- century America, or the industrial innovations that came about in nineteenth- century England, or the rise of the Nazis in twentieth- century Germany. Will such outcomes be experienced again by human societies? Probably not—and certainly not in the same way. The growing collective consciousness of and radicalization of Muslims from the later twentieth century is another such historical trend, one that is associated with fractured globalization.

The fractured manner in which globalization is taking place has resulted in serious threats to certain basic needs, particularly identity needs, of fundamentalist Muslims in particular. In the next two chapters the focus is on, first, globalization as it is supposed to take place according to certain ideals and, second, fractured globalization as it is actually taking place. Thus, the next two chapters set the context in which fundamentalist Muslims in particular experience threats to their basic needs.

CHAPTER 4

One World: Globalization as Ideal

The worldly hope men set their heart upon
Turns ashes—or it prospers; and anon,
Like snow upon the desert's dusty face
Lighting up a little hour or two—is gone.
                    —Omar Khayam (c.1048–c.1122)

"My name is Ozymandias, king of kings:
Look on my works, ye Mighty, and despair!"
Nothing beside remains. Round the decay
Of that colossal wreck, boundless and bare
The lone and level sands stretch far away.
                    —Percy Shelley (1792–1822)

At the heart of the argument for "one world" is the common human condition, the deep existential experience of each of us being on this earth for only a brief period. Ultimately, we are bound together by our transience, and the anxiety-provoking experience of living always with the knowledge of certain death ahead of us. The old saying that we can only be sure of two things, "death and taxes" needs revision as many multimillionaires manage to escape taxes, but not even the wiliest of accountants that money can buy are able to do creative accounting tricks that cheat death. Again and again, the poets remind us of this predicament, telling us that even those who become "king of kings" cannot defy death, and eventually end up returning to "desert sands." "Mighty leaders" can, for a brief period, warn others to "Look on my works... and despair!" but time will render even the greatest leader powerless.

In addition to our shared experience of transience, a common ancestry is proposed for us by the major religions as well as by science—a rare instance when science and religion agree on an important matter. According to Christian, Islamic, and Jewish traditions, all humans are descended from the same source and created by God. From this religious perspective, all humans trace their history to Adam and Eve and their banishment from the Garden of Eden. Scientific accounts of our origins, shaped by Charles Darwin's evolutionary theory, also emphasize our common roots. Scientific evidence suggests we evolved from the same sources as all other living organisms. From the same "simple" origins, our ancestors very gradually branched off in a different direction, started walking on two feet about 5 million years ago, then developed language abilities and established settlements and farms. In a literal sense, then, we share not only the same fleeting experience on this earth in our individual lives, but also the same evolutionary origins in our collective lives.

OUR COMMON ORIGINS AND SHARED COLLECTIVE CHALLENGE

Our common origins are an important source of inspiration for supporters of globalization and the movement to achieve a "global village." For these globalization supporters, the challenge is to return to perceiving ourselves to be, and acting as, one group. What better than to overcome the barriers that keep us from becoming one unbroken human society, setting aside divisions based on nationality, religion, race, and language? What better than to once again see ourselves as one humankind, without artificial divisions to separate us and serve as a basis of conflict and war? After all, the national groupings that have formed the basis of coalitions in the two world wars are merely artificial constructions. The maps of nation states can be redrawn in infinite different ways. Unified, we can take on what the Turkish–American researcher Muzafer Sherif (1906–1988) called *superordinate goals*, goals that all groups want to achieve but that no group can achieve without cooperation from other groups.[1]

Most of the countries of the Near and Middle East have borders that were drawn up by colonial representatives at the start of the twentieth century, and "feelings of nationalism" in the region are tied to borders that might be redrawn again without going against much history. This fact is unfortunately often overlooked. For example, after the 2003 invasion of Iraq by the United States and its allies, there was insistence that

Iraq be held together and not be allowed to break up into independent Shi'a, Sunni, and Kurdish states. However, even though human civilization first began in the Near East region, the Iraq nation state is a recent construction, with newly created borders. There is no historic reason why the colonial-inspired map of modern Iraq should not be redrawn into three parts.

Advances in transportation and communication mean that all of us on earth can truly feel and act as one human society. We can instantly share the happiness and misfortunes of others across the other side of the world. If there is a famine or earthquake or some other natural disaster, we can immediately share the pain of victims in other continents and send them aid, as we would help others in our own village or town. Technology can make us aware of distress experienced by people living continents away, as if they are our own kin living next door.

Support for "one world" and the assimilation of people into one human group is in line with empirical research demonstrating commonalities across groups. Despite the stereotypes often used in everyday life, reflecting exaggerations about intergroup differences, there are also some important similarities across all humans. For example, men and women are very similar on many key psychological characteristics, with a very small subset of women and men being different and not falling in the same normal distribution. Similarly, one could argue that with respect to basic psychological characteristics, there are some important continuities across cultural groups.

UNIVERSALS AGAIN: THE SPECIAL ROLE OF EMPATHY

I am returning to the topic of universals in behavior because of the profound importance of this topic. The so-called "war on terror" has further balkanized the world, placing humans in different groups that are assumed to be different from one another. The "terrorists and the societies they come from" are assumed to be completely different from "us and our societies." This trend has led to assumed differences across human groups to be highlighted, and similarities and continuities to be neglected. But in order to understand and defeat terrorism, it is essential that we appreciate the characteristics that humans have in common, particularly our basic needs, and the consequences of threats to basic needs.

Earlier (in Chapter 3) I discussed turn-taking and trust as examples of universals, which evolved as primitive social behaviors, essential building blocks of human social life, early on in human evolution.[2] Both turn-taking and trust are learned early in human development, starting with the relationship of the infant with a caretaker (typically the mother). Infants learn to turn take in feeding and resting, and in communicating with a caretaker. The roots of adult interpersonal trust are also in this infant–caretaker relationship.

A case can be made that empathy is another behavioral universal, but depends less on learning. Newborn infants cry at the sound of another infant's cries.[3] This "instinctive" reaction serves as a basis for an essential wider social role for empathy: there has to be a minimal level of empathy in relationships between the members of a society in order for that society to survive. In everyday life, functional societies are such that empathy leads individuals to help one another in times of difficulty. For example, when there is a natural disaster (such as an earthquake, flood, or fire), the experience of empathy leads to helping behavior, at least to an extent that enables the victims of catastrophe to regroup and become a functional part of society once again. To take another example, when people witness an automobile accident, or house fire, or a robbery, or some form of violent crime, they typically empathize with the victim and try to help.

Even though it is not the duty of individual citizens to show empathy and try to help the victims of accidents, such behavior is lauded. Of relevance in this context is the distinction between ordinary duty, what a person owes others in a society, and *supererogatory duties*, what a person is not obligated to carry out, but is applauded for carrying out. For example, if Joe is walking along a riverbank and he sees a child fall into the fast flowing waters of the river, he is not duty bound to dive in, risk his own life, in order to try to save the child. However, if Joe does dive in, he is fulfilling a supererogatory duty and will be applauded (particularly if he manages to save the child).

There are also *supererogatory rights*, what a person is owed by others, but is willing to forgo for the sake of a greater good. For example, Joe has a right to publish information about an impending government military operation against a terrorist group, but decides not to exercise this right in order to safeguard the operation.

Thus, a strong argument for assimilation is that humans are essentially similar in some key respects, that empathy and other universals form the building blocks for a "global village," and it is only natural that we merge into one world. Although under present conditions we learn to be more empathic toward those who share our characteristics (for example, in terms of race, religion, and other group memberships), this is not how we start life as infants. A six-month-old infant cries in response to the cries of another infant, irrespective of whether the other infant is born as Christian, Muslim, or Jewish. We could be socialized to show a different pattern of empathy as adults. I begin by noting that assimilation into "one world" can come about through government policy as well as through market forces. Next, I consider a range of vital reasons why assimilation into one world and one humankind should bring advantages.

GOVERNMENTS, MARKETS, AND ASSIMILATION INTO ONE WORLD

Among the various groups of idealists who believe that history involves a "progressive" march toward the achievement of one unified, assimilated world, two groups warrant our particular attention because of their enormous global influence, their zeal, their complete opposition to one another, as well as their both being completely wrong in their basic assumptions and predictions. One of these groups follows a Marxist ideology and the second a capitalist ideology, demonstrating nicely how being completely wrong is not exclusive to left or right political leanings.

Karl Marx (1818–1883) lived for much of his productive adult life in total obscurity and utter poverty in exile in London, England, where he died and was buried. At the time of his death, it seemed only a remote possibility that his ideas would inspire vast, international revolutionary movements and even a remoter possibility that governments, societies, and empires would claim to be shaped by his views. By the mid-twentieth century, the Soviet empire, communist China, and dozens of lesser states claimed Marxism as their economic, political, and cultural foundation. Marxism came to rival Christianity, Islam, Judaism, and other major religions in its ability to inspire enormous collective movements around the world.

The reason why Marxism has had global impact comparable to the major religions is simply because, like all religions, Marxism is based on blind faith about a particular "inevitable" utopian future. Just as the major religions demand that the faithful must believe in unproven and unprovable futures, such the afterlife, heaven, hell, and so on, Marxism demands that the faithful believe in a unified "global village" in the shape of a classless society, a society that does not need a central government. Just as religious visions of heaven tend to reflect the kinds of features that the earthly faithful daydream about in their everyday lives—luxurious places to live, endless supplies of delicious food, splendid health, beautiful people, and so on—so the Marxist paradise conjures up exactly the kinds of "heavenly" scenes that the working faithful daydream about as they march through the drudgery of their labor, that is to say, a world of both equality and plenty, with everyone being their own bosses and not being told what to do by authoritarian employers.

Marx as a Religious Prophet

The vision presented by Marx, a vision as inspired and heavenly as any experienced by religious prophets, involves a step by step progression toward a unified world, a utopian global village where all humans enjoy equality and freedom as members of one enormous collectivity.[4] Received wisdom tells us that Marx is a materialist, and this is true in the sense that Marx assumes that material conditions shape social and psychological experiences. However, being a materialist does not make Marx a realist nor does it prevent him from making predictions about the future of the world based on blind faith—a faith as blind and as powerful as any religious zealot ever experienced.

Like any paradise, the road to the Marxist paradise requires sacrifice and trials and tribulations. The people have to first go through many hardships and conflicts in order to arrive at a realization about what really matters in this world (according to Marx, that is). The revelation people finally arrive at is that in the capitalist system the only thing that matters is social class divisions. All other forms of groupings, such as those based on gender or race for example, are secondary and misleading because they divert attention away from social class. After this revelation is achieved and the people now see the truth, then the lower class (the "proletariat") confront, fight, and eventually defeat the capitalists, the "upper class" (the ones who own the "means of production"). After the capitalists have been defeated, there is only one class left standing, and a dictatorship governs in favor of everyone. Step by step, life in this proletariat dictatorship changes how people think and act, so they learn to work for each other and to achieve satisfaction by sacrificing for the collective interest rather than their (selfish) personal interest.

In a world in which every individual sees themselves as members of one large group, works for the good of everyone, and is motivated to improve the lot of all society, what purpose is served by a central government? No purpose at all, argues Marx. Central governments are only there to maintain the power and resource monopoly of the ruling class. When there is no ruling class, there is no need for a central government. Consequently, the central government dissolves and eventually disappears.

In a strange sense, then, Marxists and libertarians (and various groups of ultraconservatives) seek the same destiny for central governments: dissolution and disappearance (of course there are varieties of libertarianism[5]). However, for the libertarians the end of a central government will mean an open society in which individuals will freely compete and the realization of personal ambitions and talents will lead to differences in resources and status between individuals. From this perspective, the end of the central government is the start of a process of change, resulting in greater freedom and inequalities based on talent and motivation; it is the condition required for freedom and personal actualization to be realized. On the other hand, for Marxists the dissolution and disappearance of a central government is the final outcome of a process of gradual liberation from oppressions arising from class divisions. The central government can safely and finally be set aside when within each citizen there has evolved an adequate "conscience," a *superego* in Freudian terms, that will lead individuals to think and act according to the dictum "one for all and all for one."

Marxism in Practice

Moving from theory to practice, from ideal to actuality, has proven to be extremely difficult, if not impossible. Writing in his diaries on September 1, 1889 (well before the 1917 Russian revolution which eventually brought the communists to power and led to the creation of the Soviet Union), in a letter written on September 1, 1889, Leo Tolstoy (1828–1910) put the problem in this way:

> The most profitable arrangement of people (economic and every other) is the one in which each person thinks of the good of everyone, and unselfishly devotes himself to the service of that good. Given such an attitude on the part of everyone, each person will get the maximum share of the good. But this striving for the good of everyone is lacking among people; on the contrary, every person strives for his own good to the detriment of others; but this arrangement is so unprofitable that the struggle causes many people to weaken before long. And by the very nature of things it comes about that one man subdues others and makes them serve him... But with this... goes inequality and oppression.[6]

When Tolstoy states that "by the very nature of things it comes about that one man subdues others and makes them serve him...," is he depicting an unbending feature of human nature? Or, is he simply identifying a cultural trend that can be changed through socialization? Critics contend that it is the former, because no major society has as yet trained its citizens so that "each person thinks of the good of everyone, and unselfishly devotes himself to the service of that good."

In practice, then, the Marxist solution turns out to be no solution at all when the elite who are supposed to govern the dictatorship of the proletariat in the interests of the proletariat, only govern in their own selfish interests. As a consequence, the dictatorship of the proletariat turns into a dictatorship in favor of a pampered elite, as happened in the former Soviet Union and the former Soviet Block countries. For example, in Romania, the corrupt and despised communist dictator Nicolae Ceauşescu (1918–1989) ruled the country with an iron fist from 1965 to 1989, bringing the Romanian economy to ruins, but treating his own family and allies to a lavish "aristocratic" lifestyle. History has demonstrated that a dictatorship of the government "on behalf of the people" does not lead to "one world" and the eventual dissolution of the government; rather, it leads to deep but camouflaged class-based divisions, and movement in directions other than "one world characterized by equality and freedom."

Worse still, as is made clear by criticisms raised in the writings of Karl Popper[7] and others, because Marxist society is closed rather than open, the "pampered elite" literally get away with murder. Of course, it could be argued that such a "pampered elite" would not be in power in a real Marxist society, but how do we know when we arrive at such a state?

The Marxist solution to the utopian "one world" runs into a version of the chicken and egg problem. In order to arrive at the classless society, a dictatorship of the proletariat has to be established and "representatives of the people" have to govern in the interests of the people. But wherever we look in communist societies the experience has been the same: the "representatives of the people" use their power to further their own interests and to repress the people, so society never makes real progress toward the dissolution and disappearance of the central government and the development of a classless society. On the contrary, the "representatives of the people" use their power to set themselves up as the ruling class and to increase the distance between themselves and the rest. In practice, it turns out that the "representatives of the people" have never managed to develop the kind of psychological characteristics needed to avoid monopolizing power and resources for themselves and repressing the rest of society.

A number of modern theories, such as social dominance theory, focus on the inequalities and stratification that characterizes all human societies.[8] There is evidence to suggest that some individuals are more supportive of inequalities, and see it as natural that there be gulfs between the "rulers" and the "ruled." But it is not at all clear if stratification and inequality is an inherent part of human societies, or if it is possible to change ourselves so that equality rather than inequality becomes the norm. In addition, if we are condemned to live in societies characterized by inequalities, how can we ensure greater fairness?

How does one ensure that those who rule in the name of the people do not abuse their power and position? Plato placed his faith in education and training: create a special group of philosopher kings who would not be motivated by greed for power and resources, and would have the right kind of moral and intellectual strength to rule wisely. I also have faith in the power of education and training to create the right kinds of rulers, but that is not enough. Also needed are strong laws ensuring freedom of expression, a vibrant and critical press, and open access to information.

The Market as Creator of "One World"

An alternative to the Marxist vision of a unified, classless global village, with no central government, is a capitalist vision of a stratified global village, welded together through free trade and mutual interests. In its pure and radical form, the capitalist vision of an ideal "one world" is in important respects very similar to the Marxist vision. For example, both the capitalist and the Marxist idealized "one worlds" involve either minimal or no central government at all. As we shall see, however, the path to the unified capitalist and Marxist unified "one worlds" is very different.

The capitalist vision of a unified global village has diverse roots and strands, but a common theme is to demonstrate the triumph of capitalism and liberal democracy over communism and socialist ideologies generally. It is no surprise, then, to find that a book celebrating western liberal democracy as the "end of history" would be received with wild enthusiasm by supporters of capitalism. What better publicity in support of western capitalist countries than a book arguing that these countries have reached the penultimate point in history, that they have arrived at the *final form of human government*? Before we return to the implausible idea that history has an "end point," it is useful to review the different roots of the capitalist vision of a unified global village.

A first theme is the assumed social and political benefits of international free trade and economic integration, an idea first championed by the nineteenth- century *Manchester School* of economic thought. According to this viewpoint, free trade leads to the development of one huge global market, with labor, capital, and goods and services moving around to take maximum advantage of market conditions. As a consequence of the free market, there emerges increasing specialization of activities so that each unit focuses on producing those products for which they have a competitive edge. As a consequence, free trade can lead to greater efficiency, specialization, and productivity, but also increasing interdependence between different groups, regions, and states. For example, in the modern context, when two countries, such as the United States and China, rely heavily on one another for trade, they are far less likely to wage war against each other.

Thus, according to this economic perspective, international free trade has two sets of very clear advantages. First, market efficiency leads to lower prices and better utilization of labor and other resources to maximize production. Productivity increase leads to a "trickle down" effect and eventually raises the standard of living for everyone. Second, because it is good for business and in the interests of all groups, everyone has a strong incentive to maintain peaceful relations and avoid war.

The Capitalist Version of "No Central Government"

In the ideal capitalist scenario, the government does not interfere in trade and allows the free movement of goods and people according to supply and demand. The role of the government is minimized to maintaining peace and security. But because of complete economic interdependence between peoples around the world and the disappearance of national borders, the need for large armies disappears. Economic interests unify the world and dissolve the central governments of the "old" states. The same trends dissolve the United Nations and other international agencies: when the world is one unified free market and national governments with their expensive standing military forces have faded away, there is no need for United Nations "world government" type organizations.

Related to the economic argument for "one world" is a sociopolitical argument that, like Marxism, sees historical progression, but in this case transformation toward a stratified liberal democracy, rather than a classless society. This version of the "end of history" thesis can be supported by citing a wide array of events over the last few centuries, including the American and French revolutions of the late eighteenth century, the parliamentary reforms of 1832 in England, the 1848 revolutions throughout Europe, and the expansion of democratic movements throughout the world in the twentieth century, culminating in the "democratization" of states that made up the former Soviet Union from

1989. One might argue that the twenty-first century has seen the same "democratizing" trend, including in Iraq, Afghanistan, and other Near and Middle Eastern societies.

This capitalist version of the "end of history" thesis is religiously propagated by its supporters as fervently as is the Marxist version of the "end of history" thesis by its own supporters. Supporters of the capitalist version of the "end of history" thesis claim that the capitalist route allows far greater freedom and openness. However, in essence both the capitalist and Marxist routes to "the end of history" are closer to closed systems, in the sense that they insist that they have arrived at the end of historical development and that transformations in political, economic, and social structures will end when their particular ideal forms are achieved. In essence, a capitalist vision of history ending in a free-market liberal democracy across the world is just as "closed" and unlikely as is a Marxist vision of history ending in a classless society. In practice, the "free and open market" is as unlikely as the classless society—both ideals are rendered impossible by the tendency for humans to monopolize power, and to create favored in-groups and elites. Rather than an inevitable "progress" toward capitalist democracies, the course of human history remains unpredictable and open, and will only end when humankind becomes extinct.

PSYCHOCULTURAL ARGUMENTS FOR ONE WORLD

Why should we believe that assimilation into one unified world will be better for us? A simple answer is that we should believe because science says so. Since at least the 1930s, social science research has provided evidence and arguments in favor of the melting away of intergroup differences toward the development of one assimilated, unified world. The relevant arguments and evidence can be divided into two categories: first, evidence suggesting that assimilation is made inevitable by such factors as increased contact (as brought about by globalization, for example); second, evidence that assimilation has beneficial outcomes for humankind.

Assimilation as Inevitable

The idea that assimilation is inevitable arises from two sources, the first is trends in the United States and other immigrant-receiving societies, and the second is trends more directly associated with globalization.

In 1909 a play entitled *The Melting Pot*[9] became a success in New York, showing scenes of life in the United States, "God's crucible," where all the races were melted and reshaped to form a single great people, the Americans, with a brand new culture, the American culture. The experiences of immigrants in the United States and other immigrants receiving societies provide a model for assimilation more broadly. Immigrants come from a wide range of national, ethnic, linguistic, religious, racial, and cultural backgrounds, and through participation in one open American market and society, their differences eventually melt away and they become assimilated into one society, one people, with one common language and culture.

The idea that continuous contact between people with widely different characteristics would eventually lead to assimilation and the melting away of differences has been formalized under the title of the *contact hypothesis*. The American researcher Gordan Allport (1897–1967) was the first to systematically try to identify the conditions necessary for intergroup contact to lead to benefits.[10] Such conditions are thought to be necessary because contact in some circumstances obviously do not lead to greater liking between groups and the melting away of intergroup differences. For example, slaves and slave owners can have a lot of contact, but the outcome of such contact might not be at all beneficial to the slaves, or lead to closer ties or greater similarities, or greater mutual liking, between slaves and slave owners.

Over the last half century a lot of research has been done to test the role of the conditions identified by Allport and others as important in arriving at the assumed benefits of intergroup contact. For example, research shows some support for the idea that intergroup contact is more likely to lead to positive outcomes when such contact is supported by the larger society, when the two groups involved share certain common goals, when the context of the intergroup contact is cooperative rather than competitive, and when the two groups have about equal status. These seem to be very difficult conditions to meet, so one might become pessimistic about contact leading to positive benefits. For example, consider how difficult it would be to create situations in which minority and majority groups first enjoy equal status (as a precondition for contact leading to positive outcomes). Fortunately, when Tom Pettigrew reviewed hundreds of studies and assessed the overall trend, his conclusion is that contact has positive benefits independent of the detailed conditions in which contact takes place.

Consequently, the picture seems to be fairly positive: as long as we bring groups together long enough, so that they have continuous intergroup contact over a long time, liking and similarity between groups will tend to increase. The broad trend of the research suggests that contact can be enough.

Varieties of Assimilation

But we still need to make some policy decisions about the kind of assimilation we want to achieve. Let us call the first type of assimilation *minority-group assimilation*: this takes place when minority groups change to become more like the majority group. For example, immigrants to the United States change to become culturally more like the white majority group. The second type of assimilation better fits the label *melting-pot assimilation*, because all the groups change, each melting a little and each contributing to a completely new group that emerges. The result is a new society and a new people, different from all the groups that originally contributed to the "melting pot."

An argument can be made that melting-pot assimilation is more in line with democratic principles than is minority-group assimilation. This is because in melting-pot assimilation, all the different minority and majority groups contribute toward the development of a new culture, and so every culture "has a say" in shaping the culture that eventually emerges. Although this argument has some merit, it has a fatal flaw, because in practice the more powerful groups have "more of a say." In essence, even in melting-pot assimilation, some cultures are more equal than others.

Historically, assimilation in the United States has taken place through a mixture of melting-pot and minority-group assimilation processes, with some regional variations as to which one is more prominent. For example, in the greater Miami and Los Angeles regions, Latinos have experienced melting-pot assimilation, and they have contributed in substantial ways to the local culture (the same is true for South Asians in parts of Birmingham, Manchester, and some other cities in England; for Turks in parts of Hamburg and other German cities; North Africans in parts of Paris, in France, and so on). However, in Minneapolis and some other American cities, Hispanics have (so far) followed more of a minority-assimilation path, in part because their numbers have remained too small to do otherwise.

Parallel to the argument that the assimilation of immigrants in the United States and other immigrant-receiving countries is inevitable, there runs an argument that assimilation is made inevitable by globalization. At both national and global levels, it is assumed that gigantic economic and technological forces (such as the ever expanding power and reach of computers) will lead people to assimilate and become more like one another in culture and lifestyle. Symbolic of these assimilation changes, and a motor driving them, is assimilation in language. In the last five hundred years the number of living languages has decreased by about

60 percent.[11] Hundreds of languages only have one or two speakers left, and several languages become extinct each month. By the end of the twenty-first century, most of the languages still alive today will be extinct. Just as minority languages are disappearing, a small number of "majority languages" (particularly Mandarin Chinese, English, Spanish) are becoming more and more dominant. Over 90 percent of humankind now speak one or several of about ten languages (this topic is discussed further in Chapter 6).

Language death is a direct result of fractured globalization. Huge inequalities and disparities between groups thrown into sudden contact means that the languages of some (minority) groups will perish and the language of other (majority) groups will become more dominant. Because language is an enormously important carrier of culture and worldview, a group that has lost its language is more likely to also lose its distinct culture and worldview. By taking on the language of majority groups, minority groups also tend to adopt the worldview of majority groups.

But language loss is not necessarily negative; becoming one unified global village is seen as having tremendous benefits, a topic we turn to next.

Assimilation as Beneficial

What is your idea of utopia, the ideal world? Most people have responded to this question by describing a world that is (among other things) unified and peaceful, a place where there are minimal divisions and conflict, and where everyone is treated first and foremost as a human being, rather than as a member of a particular group. Assimilation into one global village seems to be one way to achieve these aspects of utopia.

Assimilation is seen to make us more similar to one another, and this must be considered as part of the benefits of assimilation into "one world."

The Powerful Benefits of Similarity

Imagine a world in which everyone has similar values and a similar lifestyle, a world in which people think of themselves as belonging to the same in-group—humankind. Imagine a world in which we understand one another better, because we all speak the same language. Similarity might have a few (some would suggest relatively minor) disadvantages, but social science research suggests it can have huge advantages.

Both at the interpersonal and intergroup levels similarity is associated with attraction. In friendship and love, similarity has a powerful impact:

we typically are more inclined to make friends with and to fall in love with others who are more similar to us.[12] Although in Hollywood movies there are lots of tales about how two totally dissimilar individuals fall in love, in real life dissimilarity-attraction is uncommon and it is similarity that wins out. This is true for both modern romantic love where the two lovers "freely" choose one another, and in arranged marriages that continue to be customary in some traditional communities.

In preparing for an arranged marriage, families in traditional communities typically give a great deal of importance to similarity. Matchmakers consider criteria such as the status and financial situation of each of the families, as well as the background, age, and characteristics of the bride and bridegroom. The objective of matchmakers is to bring together a couple who are similar, and their assumption is that similarity will lead to a successful marriage, both for the man and woman, as well as for their respective families.

The power of similarity-attraction is also evident in organizations.[13] Individuals looking for work are attracted to organizations that "fits" their personality characteristics. Correspondingly, in their selection of new employees, organizations tend to prefer individuals who are more similar to and fit in with their corporate culture. Of course, as employees stay longer in an organization, they tend to change and conform to organizational norms, thus becoming more similar to one another in attitudes, judgments, and so on. This process results in a more cohesive, well-coordinated team. Of course, too much conformity can also stifle creativity.

Similarity-Attraction in Intergroup Relations

In addition to research demonstrating that similarity is associated with attraction and more positive attitudes and actions at the interpersonal level, there is evidence that similarity has a similar impact at the intergroup level. In court cases, there is evidence that jurors are more lenient toward accused defendants who are similar to them in terms of ethnicity or gender, or both.[14] But what happens in societies that celebrate cultural diversity, where each group is encouraged to maintain its heritage culture? In a context of "celebrating differences," does similarity-attraction still work? Do group members still feel more inclined to interact with more similar others? In order to address these questions, I helped conduct a study on intergroup relations in Canada.

The Canadian context is very suitable for such a study because Canada was the first nation to officially adopt a multicultural policy, introduced by the Canadian Prime Minister Pierre Trudeau (1919–2000) in 1972.

Trudeau was a naturally charismatic leader, the kind that comes along in a country once every century. Through his magnetic influence, Canadians were persuaded to adopt a policy of "multiculturalism within a bilingual framework." The primary goal of this policy was to keep the French and the English wedded to one united Canada, but also to celebrate the many different cultural groups in Canada. The federal government of Canada has given support to ethnic groups to maintain and celebrate their cultural and linguistic characteristics, and to share their heritage cultures with other groups. In this context, where intergroup differences are being highlighted and celebrated, is there still a tendency for people to prefer similar outgroups?

In order to examine this question, I collaborated in a study carried out in Canada, with samples from four minority groups (Algerian, Indian, Jewish, and Greek) and the two Canadian majority groups (English Canadian and French Canadian).[15] We explored the relationship between (1) how similar the members of each minority and majority groups saw the members of the other groups to be to their group, and (2) how willing the members of each minority and majority group were to interact with others (for example, how willing they were to have the members of other groups be their colleagues at work, or their neighbors, or marry into their families). The results of the study show a strong pattern of association between similarity and attraction: the more an outgroup member was seen to be similar, the more a person desired to interact with that outgroup member. This pattern of similarity-attraction held constant across the different minority and majority groups.

Implication of Similarity-Attraction for Policy

An implication of similarity-attraction research is that we should be supporting a policy of assimilation leading to a more homogeneous society, with greater similarity between people, rather than supporting a multicultural policy that "celebrates differences" and highlights dissimilarity. Moreover, in an era when the "spread of democracy" around the globe is a major objective (at least as far as the rhetoric of western and particularly American politicians is concerned), then we should be concerned about the possible detrimental impact of diversity on democracy. Some have argued that democracy is more difficult to establish and maintain in ethnically diverse societies.[16]

An example of how ethnic diversity might present challenges for democracy is found in elections in Iraq after the 2003 invasion by the United States and its allies. Instead of voting along ideological lines, with allegiances to different political parties formed according to political principles, Iraqis voted along ethnic lines. For the most part, Shi'a Muslims voted for Shi'a candidates, Sunni (non-Kurdish) Muslims either did not vote or voted for Sunni (non-Kurdish) candidates, and Kurds voted for Kurdish candidates. In this case, instead of healing rifts and helping to unify the country, "democratic elections" increased divisions and pushed Iraq further along the path of fragmentation. This is another argument for following a policy of assimilation, rather than celebrating and strengthening diversity.[17]

Assimilation and the Meritocratic Ideal

"Equality of opportunity," "fair play," "a level playing field"—these are the kinds of phrases that come to mind when most people imagine a just society. The notion that everyone should have an equal chance at working hard, using their talents, becoming successful, and moving up the status hierarchy. Those who are dedicated and talented should move ahead, that is accepted as part of a meritocracy. But the question remains, under what conditions does a meritocracy best come into effect? Does meritocracy best flourish in a situation where multiculturalism is put into effect, intergroup differences are celebrated, and groups are encouraged to maintain and strengthen their distinct ways of life? Or is meritocracy best served by an assimilationist policy, where the focus is on similarities, and people are encouraged to set aside their differences?

A strong case can be made for the position that meritocracy has the best opportunity to become realized through a policy of assimilation. This is because a multicultural policy leads to children from different ethnic, linguistic, religious, and cultural groups having different life experiences. This difference in life experiences is magnified by children from different groups attending different schools so that, for example, in a particular city affluent white Protestants attend school "A," affluent Catholics attend school "B," working class African Americans attend school "C," working class Hispanics attend school "D," and so on. Moreover, children belonging to different groups are socialized differently through the clubs, religious institutions, cultural organizations, and so on, of their respective groups. The outcome could be a society in which children from some groups are much more culturally literate[18] and better equipped than children from other groups to compete in mainstream society.

By educating and socializing all children using the same language and the same cultural framework, it will be possible to create a level playing field. If there are cultural biases in the standardized tests (such as the SAT, MCAT, LSAT, GRE, and so on), then the biases will not work against any particular group, because irrespective of their backgrounds children will have been similarly equipped for life in the mainstream.

Benefits of Assimilation for Women in Muslim Countries

Assimilation toward becoming "one world" has already had considerable benefits, particularly for women and other power minorities. For example, an important consequence of globalization is the spread of values such as "equality," "the right to education," "the right to have representation," and so on. A consequence is the dramatically improved performance of women in higher education. It is not only in the United States and other western societies that females are now beating out the males in university entrance examinations so that the number of female undergraduates exceeds male undergraduates. This same trend is evident in almost all non-western societies, and in some respects this shatters stereotypes. For example, consider the stereotype of young women in the Islamic Republic of Iran—covered by the Islamic veil, kept segregated, prevented from equal participation in public life, treated as second-class citizens by the legal system.

Despite the second-class status of women in contemporary Iran, globalization trends led to women in Iran being given the opportunity to compete equally for university places and, of course, there are now more women than men undergraduates in Iranian universities. This came about through policies introduced by the Shah in the late 1960s, with the intention of bringing Iranian higher education in line with at least some aspects of global international trends. After women were encouraged to participate as equals in the university entrance examinations, the number of women in Iranian higher education increased. This trend continued after the 1978–1979 revolution, and now Iranian women, like women in other non-western societies, have shown that when given an opportunity to compete on equal terms, they can get ahead of the men.[19] This is an example of what I consider to be the benefits of globalization. However, on the dark side, globalization has a number of serious detrimental consequences, considered in the next chapter.

CONCLUDING COMMENT

There are numerous important reasons why we should look favorably on globalization. From the perspective of both left-wing and right-wing utopians, the best possible world is one in which national, ethnic, and other such boundaries evaporate and we come to live in a world without borders. This idealist vision of "one world" has been lauded by various poets, writers, and artists throughout the ages. The so-called "CNN effect" means that we become immediately aware of events in distant places, and can feel empathic toward the plight of others who we never meet directly.[20]

If globalization takes place in an ideal way, then there would be less threat to the basic human needs of certain groups. However, in practice we are living in the age of fractured globalization, and a consequence is that some groups experience threatened identities as well as attacks on some of their other basic human needs. In the next chapter, we turn to consider fractured globalization in more detail.

Of course there is heated disagreement about the nature of globalization, in part because we are in the midst of globalization changes and it is still difficult to recognize what we are experiencing. Part of the difficulty arises from the multiple nature of globalization: the globalization that people in New York, Washington (DC) London, Paris, and Berlin experience is very different from the globalization that people in many other parts of the world experience. This is part of the nature of fractured globalization.

CHAPTER 5

Fractured Globalization: Globalization in Practice

Things fall apart; the centre cannot hold
Mere anarchy is loosed upon the world.
—William Butler Yeats (1865–1939)[1]

"...the globalization project is in crisis...We have...entered a historical maelstrom marked by prolonged economic crisis, the spread of global resistance, the reappearance of the balance of power among centre states, and the re-emergence of acute inter-imperialist contradictions."

—Walden Bello[2]

"About 2.7 billion people, or over half the developing world's population, live on less that $2 a day...At the other end of the spectrum, in 2006 the world has 293 billionaires with a combined wealth of $2.6 trillion—equivalent to 20 per cent of the United States' annual gross domestic product (GDP)...in 2006...an average billionaire could have hired nearly 2 million of these (the poorest half of the worlds') workers."

—Homer-Dixon[3]

The ideal of globalization implies the development of a cohesive world, one in which there is greater togetherness, openness, and prosperity for all. Open global markets and increased international trade are supposed to create new wealth for humankind. Even though this wealth is assumed to be unequally distributed, a "trickle-down" effect is supposed to spread the wealth to everyone, including the poorest groups. All boats will be lifted by the rising tide, that is what received wisdom tells us.

In practice, globalization is characterized by enormous contradictions, inequalities, and conflicts. Although vast wealth is being created, this has increased rather than decreased inequalities around the world. The situation in the United States was captured by a headline in *The New York Times* in March 2007, "The Greatest U.S. Income Inequality Since the Depression."[4] Research by the epidemiologist Michael Marmot[5] shows that income disparities have concrete health consequences. Societies with greater income inequalities risk paying a high price because of detrimental health consequences experienced by those people who are relatively poor.

Relative wealth is often even more important than absolute wealth. If Michael earns three dollars a day and most people in his society earn two dollars a day, Michael feels very different about his status compared to when he earns three dollars a day but most people in his society earn three hundred dollars a day. Research by Marmot and others suggests that the vast majority of people benefit from living in societies where income disparities are less rather than more, where income disparities are more like that of the Scandinavian countries than in the United States.

Globalization has increased income inequalities in many parts of the world so that the poor are not only left further behind, but they also feel relatively more deprived. This increased fraternal relative deprivation has come about through the global reach of advertising, television, and "Hollywood style" entertainment generally. The globalization of advertising and Hollywood-style media means that poor people in the farthest corners of the globe become influenced by the affluent middle-class lifestyle. Images of affluence and success reach the world's poor and contradict their harsh everyday experiences.

The greatest contradiction, and the one that has been almost completely ignored, arises from the competing pull of technological, economic, and political forces on the one hand and psychological factors on the other hand.

GLOBAL ECONOMY, LOCAL IDENTITY

Technological, economic, and political forces are pushing individuals to be part of larger and larger units, toward the global, but our psychosocial needs are pulling us to remain wedded to smaller units, toward the local.[6]

The Technological Push Toward Global

When Jules Verne published his novel *Around the World in Eighty Days* (*Le tour du monde en quatre-vingts jours*) in 1873, it was a great challenge to circumnavigate the world in eighty days, even using the most advanced transportation of the day. In our time, rockets can zoom around planet earth in a few hours. Whereas in 1873 relatively few people routinely traveled internationally, in the twenty-first century millions of travelers are transported across continents each year. Revolutionary changes in transportation technology have opened the floodgates to millions of people traveling around the globe, mostly in fairly high comfort.

Those who are unable or do not wish to physically travel can go on virtual tours using "computer travel," and they can be in touch with other people in different countries using e-mail and other electronic communications systems. Indeed, the e-mail system is now one of the strongest mechanisms pushing us toward the global, changing our social relationships. It is not unusual now for people to maintain close relationships with others thousands of miles away, through e-mail, videoconferencing, the telephone, and other electronic means of communications. At the same time that we can now be intimate with others who are physically continents away from us, we might not even know the names of people living right next door to us.

Electronic communications have given us virtual friends and intimates. Through chat rooms, blogs, You Tube, and other such means, twenty-first- century humans develop relationships with others who they might never meet and whose real names they might never know. These others are often in distant lands they will probably never visit.

The Economic Push Toward Global

When Adam Smith published his monumental work *An Inquiry Into The Nature and Causes of the Wealth of Nations*[7] in 1776, the economic push toward globalization had already been launched. England, Spain, France, Portugal, and other western powers of the time had already begun the colonization of Asia, Africa, and America. Australia had been "discovered" (in 1768) by the British explorer Captain James Cook (1728–1779) and new trade routes were being explored in the farthest distances of the globe. The economic theories of Adam Smith and other economists of the "free trade" movement naturally led to the idea, an ideal for some thinkers, of the entire globe as a single free-trade zone.

Although we are still very far from global free trade because nation states and regions (such as the European Union) still maintain tariffs against foreign imports, we are moving closer and closer to an integrated global economy. With each passing year, a greater portion of world economic activity gets global rather than local, between nations and regions rather than within themselves. Visible signs of this are outsourcing and the spread of name brands, such as McDonalds and Pizza Hut, to the farthest corners of the globe. No part of the globe is now immune from "McDonaldization,"[8] not Beijing, not Cape Town, not Cairo, not Tel Aviv, not Caracas, and not even Paris. We can now find American fast food on the Champs Elysees.

An important part of the global economy is the growing armies of skilled and unskilled people who move from country to country, continent to continent, in search of more profitable markets in which to sell their labor. Many of the unskilled workers move across national borders illegally, such as those moving northward from Latin America through Mexico into the United States, and those moving northward from the African continent through Morocco into Spain and the European mainland. Skilled professionals also move in large numbers, but typically with legal papers and in far greater comfort. For example, managers of international corporations move with their families from Casablanca to Madrid, from Madrid to Miami, and from Miami to Caracas with little change of lifestyle. In each new location, employees of international corporations find that their purchasing power makes available the same international schools for their children, the same entertainment products (film, music, and so on), the same food to consume (including breakfast cereals for their children), and the same cars to purchase. For the affluent, the economy has always been global; their money could buy them the same lifestyle everywhere.

The Political Push toward Global

Alongside technological and economic factors pushing toward globalization are political factors. It would be too simplistic to interpret political factors as the driving force behind all technological and economic changes because often technological changes leading to economic changes are at least initiated independent of politics, although they seldom remain separate from politics for long. For example, e-mail and the World Wide Web developed first as technological breakthroughs, and their important political influences (such as the democratization of information and communications) have come about afterwards as more and more people now use computers. This is different from technological changes that came about from the start because of political motives, an example being nuclear weapons, which were developed by some nations in order to gain power over other nations.

The main political force pushing twenty-first- century humans to join larger and larger groups is associated with regionalism.[9] Although the focus remains on "planned" regions, some regions get evolved by historical accident despite attempts to prevent their development. An example is the rise of a Shi'a region, comprising Iran and the south of Iraq.[10] Despite strenuous efforts by the United States to prevent such a turn of events, the historic ties between Shi'as in Iraq and Iran are serving as a foundation on which a new Shi'a region is being developed. Another new region that might come to fruition is a "Mediterranean block" comprising all the countries that share the Mediterranean coast.

The European Union, now enlarged to twenty-seven countries, is the most significant example of an increasingly important unit, growing larger and larger with each decade that started as a much smaller regional pact. The political and economic elite of Europe are using all the levers at their disposal to move the European population to identify with Europe and to "feel" European. The European elite is being assisted in this task by trends in technology, such as electronic communications, which are also moving toward being global. However, there also powerful forces pulling people toward the local.

The Psycosocial Pull toward the Local

"Large-scale society is a coordination system that has no proper evolutionary history; in the course of human history, it is a novelty, only 6,000 to 8,000 years old. It must operate with social cognitive processes evolved for face-to-face core configurations, and the relevant processes must be "reweavable" for higher-level coordination. As in the past, humans continue to repeatedly assemble face to face groups for reproduction and survival."

—Linnda Caporael[11]

Since bipedalism first became a human characteristic over 5 million years ago, humans have experienced life almost completely in small-group contexts. As Linnda Caporael points out, large-scale societies are very new on the evolutionary landscape. As a species, we have spent almost all of our time on earth living in groups that are small enough to have face-to-face interactions with most or all members. The eminent German ethologist Irenäus Eibl-Eibesfeldt has pointed out that even to-day hunter-gathering societies speaking one language tend to number just a few hundred members.[12] Such small groups formed a stable social unit that maximized the probability of individual survival and eventually gave rise to the stable family unit that has played such a central role in our evolutionary history.[13]

Having evolved social-psychological characteristics adapted to living in small groups, we do our best to transform our lives in large-scale societies to be compatible with our social-psychological characteristics. For example, since the industrial revolution and the enormous movements of people from rural to urban areas from the eighteenth century onward, most humans have abandoned village life and now live in large cities. But even when we live in an enormous metropolis with 5 or 10, or even 15 million inhabitants, we create far smaller neighborhoods for ourselves, places we feel we belong to. Ethnic minorities typically segregate in "their own" neighborhoods, where they feel more "at home" and more protected against prejudice and discrimination.[14] Such neighborhoods might have some physical demarcations, such as major roads or buildings, but mainly they are psychological constructions, with boundaries that exist in the minds of neighborhood inhabitants rather than having actual physical borders.

Just as we psychologically and physically create "human-scale" neighborhoods in order to belong to smaller units within vast cities, we create small units within enormously large institutions and organizations. For the last few decades I have been involved with a variety of research projects in very large organizations, both national and international. For example, I was involved for about fifteen years in cultural research in a major Swiss pharmaceutical company with dozens of affiliates and tens of thousands of employees around the world.[15] Employees felt they "belonged" to the main organization, just as citizens feel they belong to a nation, but in everyday life they interacted with small units that allowed face-to-face interactions, just as citizens belong to small units (the neighborhood, the local sports club, the Parent Teacher Association, and so on) within a nation.

Large organizations cater to our needs to belong to small units by formal organizational charts that start with the "chief" of the entire organization, but work down to managers in charge of smaller and smaller groups, finally arriving at groups small enough to enable face-to-face interactions. Terrorist organizations follow the same path, with large international networks being founded on local terrorist cells that facilitate a sense of belonging among cell members. The desire to belong to a small group that gives one a sense of purpose and positive and distinct identity is a major factor attracting young men to join terrorist cells.[16]

To summarize our predicament in the twenty-first century, while identity is local, the economy is global. While evolutionary developed social practices and motivations mean that we cling to smaller groups and neighborhoods, technological, political, and economic forces push us to the global level, to larger and larger units, and a global economy idealized by, and working in favor of, the super rich.

Gigantic Challenges Associated with Fractured Globalization

Two monstrous unknowns confront humankind at the dawn of the twenty-first century: the first is global warming, and the second is globalization. What will be the consequences of global warming? Will global warming pose a serious threat to human survival? Will we be able to act in time to reduce the detrimental impacts of global warming? Despite denials on the part of sceptics, these questions are gradually being taken seriously by the general public, in both western and non-western societies. Reports of extreme weather and rising water levels are discussed and accepted by many, as evidence that human-influenced global warming really is taking place and is bringing about changes that pose a danger to humankind. The public is demanding solutions, and some politicians are showing leadership toward finding solutions (as reflected in the Kyoto agreement, not yet ratified by the United States). But questions about the second unknown, the future of globalization, are seldom seriously addressed in debates that engage the general public.

Indeed, people in the West tend to be less critical and worried about globalization. Of course, there are some complaints, particularly about job outsourcing, but western economies are seen as resilient enough to overcome problems created by outsourcing. The general tendency is to assume that the road ahead is fairly clear and the challenges under control. The consequences of globalization are not seriously or widely debated as they should be. The most important consequences of globalization are not even recognized.

One of these detrimental consequences is the rise of Islamic fundamentalism and terrorism.[17] In order to understand this relationship, it is necessary to step back and consider the "big picture," a strategy that modern social sciences, with their emphasis on specialization and narrow focus, are poorly equipped to adopt.[18] I will begin by examining some associated consequences of globalization. Because these consequences are scattered far and wide, their common source is more difficult to identify.

An important consequence of globalization is the coming together of different groups of people with little preparation for contact with unforeseen and sometimes problematic consequences.

MIGRATIONS AND THE NEW ETHNIC MIX

A German judge has stirred a storm of protest by citing the Koran in turning down a German Muslim woman's request for a speedy divorce on the ground that her husband beat her. In a ruling that underlines the tension between Muslim customs and European laws, the judge . . . noted that the couple came from a Moroccan cultural milieu, in which it is common for husbands to beat their wives. The Koran, she wrote in her decision, sanctions such physical abuse.[19]

The above report of a German judge citing the Koran in her decision about a case involving a German Muslim woman beaten by her husband, was reported in *The New York Times*. On the same page of the same newspaper was another article about Muslims in Europe, in which it was reported that,

"A French court ruled . . . in favor of a satirical weekly newspaper that faced charges brought by two Muslim groups after it published cartoons featuring the Prophet Mohammad that had caused an international uproar when a Danish newspaper published most of them."[20]

The New York Times also reported that the most Reverend Rowan Williams, Archbishop of Canterbury, stumbled into a lot of controversy by suggesting that some aspects of *Shariah*, the legal system of Islam, should be accepted for regulating the lives of Muslims in England. The attacks on the Archbishop's speech included "mocking tabloid headlines and cartoons that focused on the extreme applications of *Shariah*, like stoning to death and the amputation of hands."[21]

These reports reflect a general trend of cultural clashes, as tens of millions of people migrate from South to North America, and from Africa, Asia, and eastern to western Europe. Of course, migration has always been integral to the human experience, but the vast scale and scope of contemporary migration is completely new, as are the outcomes of these twenty-first- century migrations.

Not Assimilating in the European Union

Manchester, Birmingham, Leeds, Liverpool, Bradford, and other cities in the midlands and the north of England have experienced enormous changes over the last few centuries. The factories that were at the heart of the industrial revolution first sprung up in these cities in the eighteenth and nineteenth centuries, as did the sooty industrial slums that became home to millions of workers needed for the new factories. Displaced from the countryside because of the modernization and mechanization of farming, hordes of people moved from rural to urban areas to find work in the new factory towns. These people helped to create the distinct working-class cultures of midlands and northern England.

For three years in the early 1970s I lived in Liverpool, at a time when the "Liverpool cultural revival" still had momentum. The city center was gutted and gripped by poverty, but there were enough active musicians, painters, authors, and various other kinds of artists to help uplift spirits despite the material poverty. At that time, a small number of South Asian immigrants added to the cultural mix and enriched the city center of Liverpool, and the same was true in other cities of the midlands and northern England. But by the turn of twenty-first century, the trickle of South Asian immigrants to these northern English cities has grown to what some English people see as a dangerous, turbulent flood. According to a 2007 report in *The Times* of London, "Muhammad is now second only to Jack as the most popular name for baby boys in Britain and is likely to rise to No.1 by next year."[22]

Today, walking through parts of Bradford and some other cities in England gives one the unmistakable impression of being in regions of Muslim Asia. The same is true for some neighborhoods in large cities in Germany, where Turks have placed their cultural stamp, and again the same experience is repeated in France, but this time with North Africans setting up little Meccas.

This is one of the few times in recorded human history that such enormous migrations have taken place voluntarily and for the purpose of people selling their labor and professional skills. The scale and pace of the contemporary migrations is unprecedented. Of course, trade and travels are not new, as evidenced for example by the global travels of Vikings on their long boats and the movement of traders along the Silk Route over a thousand years ago, as well as the more recent large-scale flocking of artists, scholars, and freethinkers to Renaissance Italy. Large-scale forced migrations are also as old as human history, with conquered people being taken from their homelands and forced to serve as slaves in foreign countries. The Roman Empire depended heavily on slave labor removed from their lands of origin, as did the modern empires of Britain and America, until the nineteenth century. However, globalization has brought about changes on a new scale: the voluntary movement of hundreds of millions of people to take advantage of better economic conditions.

The globalized migrants are not motivated to change their cultures or religions. North Africans are not moving to France because they want to abandon their traditional Islamic way of life, and particularly the traditional roles of men and women in their cultures. John Bowen[23] has addressed the issue of "Why the French don't like headscarves," but the more novel and important question in the twenty-first century is, "Why Muslims in France don't care that the French do not like headscarves." The new Muslim immigrants in France, as with over 20 million Muslim immigrants in the rest of Europe, are showing a new assertiveness—they do not want to assimilate and melt away into local French, English, German, Italian, Spanish, Swedish, Norwegian, or any other European culture. Walk through neighborhoods populated by Muslims in the United Kingdom and the impression one gets is that Muslims are not rushing to take on British values and identity. Indeed, Muslims often seem to be insisting on retaining their distinctiveness. They insist on people having the right to wear their headscarves irrespective of whether or not they themselves do so.

Population Explosion among Minorities in Europe

Low religiosity, slow population growth, and feeble levels of religious activity among the major Christian groups in Europe have provided Muslims room to maneuver and grow. For example, in Britain "practicing Muslims are likely to outnumber church-attending Christians in several decades."[24] As Christian churches remain empty and stagnant, some of them are converted to serve as mosques, underlining the fact that the new South Asian immigrants have come to participate in the British economy, but not necessarily the British culture, and certainly not the Church of England or any other branch of Christianity.

The majority of twenty-first- century migrants move from one country to another for economic reasons, and at the same time assert the right to retain their different heritage religions and identities. They do not come as slaves, but as employees who are essential for the economies of the host countries. For example, many of the 45 million Hispanics in the United States have asserted their right to retain their version of Catholicism, and their heritage identities. Many of these Hispanics are also motivated to continue to speak Spanish in the United States and their impact is clearly visible in the bilingual advertising and information bulletins of New York, Miami, Los Angeles, and other major urban centers. Despite the best efforts of the *English Only Movement*, dedicated to strengthening the status of the English language and making English the official language of the United States, the influence of Spanish is growing stronger there.

The influence of Hispanics is particularly evident in the west of the United States. Whereas in 1972 about 15 percent of the children in public schools were Hispanics, by 2005 this figure had reached 37 percent. A similar trend is evident when we consider the entire non-white student population. Whereas in 1972 about 27 percent of the children in public schools in the west of the United States were non-whites, by 2005 this figure had reached 54 percent—thus, in the West, whites are now a numerical minority in pubic schools.

The picture for the entire United States shows the same trends. Whereas in 1972 white children made up 78 percent of the population in public schools, by 2006 only 58 percent of children in public schools were white. The indications are clear: within a few decades, the U.S. population will consist of a majority of non-whites. One of the consequences of these trends is a backlash against immigrants and immigration in the United States, as reflected in the heated debates around the failed immigration bill of 2007. Despite the backlash, in important respects the United States has been successful in integrating immigrants, including Muslim immigrants. A close look at regions, where there are large numbers of Muslims in the United States such as Detroit and Los Angeles, shows that Muslims are doing well in terms of educational, economic, and cultural integration. Indeed, Muslims are ahead of the general U.S. population in education level and income. It is important to look closely at the solution put into practice in the United States, and the solution being put into practice at the global level.

AMERICAN AND GLOBAL SOLUTIONS TO MANAGING DIVERSITY

The presence of enormous ethnic enclaves consisting of people who are not motivated to assimilate into the mainstream culture of the host country is not always problematic. After all, linguistic, ethnic, and religious diversity does not necessarily lead to continued conflict. Despite the Quebec nationalist movement and clashes between French separatists and Canadian government forces in the late 1960s and early 1970s, diversity has been fairly peacefully managed in North America since the early twentieth century—after the native Indians were forcibly "re-settled" by the end of the nineteenth century.

If we overlook a number of historic exceptions, the most important being mistreatment of the native people and African Americans prior to the civil rights reforms of the 1960s, it is clear that diversity in all its forms, including religious, ethnic, and linguistic diversity, has been managed fairly effectively in the United States. Anyone who doubts this only has to walk through major urban neighborhoods in the United States, that is, New York, Detroit, Miami, Los Angeles, and so on, to witness Arabs and Jews, Catholics, and Protestants, Blacks and whites, and all different kinds of people living in peace side by side. People who would be fighting one another tooth and claw in the heritage countries back home manage to live in peace in the United States. How is this achieved?

To understand the American solution to diversity, one has to look closely at a feature of life in the United States that puzzles and even repulses many: legal disputes. Even in the shelter of academic life, I have witnessed professors take legal action against one another and against their "own" universities. But, instead of being disgusted by this behavior, I have come to see it as absolutely essential for the survival of American democracy.

The Cement Needed to Bind Diverse Societies

In reality there are only two ways to create the cement needed to bring diverse groups of people together to form a cohesive and functional society, when the building blocks for such a society are different in terms of ethnicity, religion, language, and so on. The first way is to force everyone to assimilate and to "become" part of the mainstream. This is the path traditionally adopted in France and other western European societies.

This "assimilationist" path aims to develop a common culture and language, a common set of values, shared by all. The practical question becomes, what does it mean to "be British?" Does it mean one has to "pass the cricket test?" Or, one has to be fluent in English? Is this enough? What about the case of a Pakistani cricket lover who is fluent in English, but hates England enough to want to blow himself up on a double-decker bus in London? And what about the meaning of "being French," "being German," "being Italian," and so on? What exactly is the test in each of these cases?

The assimilationist path to creating the cement to bind and build society is leading Europe to multiple quandries: how do you build cement when a common set of values is not readily available? This question is problematic in England, and France, and Germany, and other western European countries because they start with the assumption that there are clear values and norms, and beliefs that constitute "being English" and "being French" and "being German" and so on. That is why they fall into the trap of coming up with "tests" such as the "cricket test."

Law as the "Cement" Binding American Society

The American solution has been very different, in part because America has not developed a cement through a common culture, shared values, norms, and so on. With one important exception, the idea of a common set of values binding different ethnic, religious, and linguistic groups together in America is a myth. The one exception is the idea of the American dream: the notion of America being a land of renewal, a place where everyone can begin again and try to make it up the system.

Instead of relying on a common set of values to bind society together, the American solution has been to develop a strong legal framework. The American cement for binding diverse groups is legal: that is why lawyers, courts, and the law in general plays a much more intimate role in the everyday lives of Americans than in the lives of Europeans. That is why disputes in America are more likely to lead to legal suits and law courts.

When English people have disputes, they seek solutions in a common set of traditions and values. When Americans have disputes, they lack common traditions and values, and so resort to the common cement of the law.

The American solution, formal law, has been effective in a geographically mobile, multicultural society with a minimum level of shared values and norms. However, this solution has the drawback of creating a litiginous society, where children learn from an early age to repeat threats such as "I'll sue you!." I have witnessed six-year-old American children make this threat.

The solution adopted by the English, French, German, and other Europeans, that of relying on a common set of traditions and values, has worked well as long as the people in a society actually share common traditions and values. However, three changes are taking place so that this condition is no longer met.

First, because the birth rate in western Europe is below the replacement level of 2.1 percent and the European population is aging, there are fewer younger workers to support a larger and larger retired population. Productivity increases are not enough to solve this crisis. Europe is forced to import labor, including from Asian and African countries.

Second, the expansion of the European Union has led to former Soviet Block societies, including Muslim communities, to become part of the "European family." Even if Turkey is not allowed entry, there is already considerable diversity (including religious diversity) in the European Union so that one experiences tremendous differences in cultures and lifestyles moving from one part of Europe to another. Travel from Sarievo to Stokholm to Bucharest to Dublin, exposes one to very different values and norms.

Increased geographical mobility is the third change that challenges the reliance of Europe on a common set of shared values as a cement to bind society. In addition to the influx of millions of refugees and immigrants from Asia, Africa, and eastern Europe, western Europeans themselves have become more geographically mobile so that many traditional local neighborhood ties are loosened. The present generation if western Europeans are more likely, than their parents, to move from place to place, both within and between countries.

As a consequence, western Europeans are increasingly sharing the "New York experience." It is a truism that in New York and other major urban centers of the United States, one can live for years next door to other people without ever coming to know who they are. The same has come true in London, Paris, Munich, Madrid, Rome, Copenhagen, Stockholm, and a number of other major western urban centers.

Thus, both the large-scale importation of labor (in the shape of immigrants and refugees) to Europe and the expansion of the European Union have resulted in the weakening of the normative cement that might bind the Europeans together. Despite the appeal of various Popes to a "common Christian heritage" in Europe, affiliation with the Christian church has proven to be too weak to serve as a cement for the European Union. The result is the increased importance of "the law" emanating from Brussels as well as the rise of legalistic thinking in Europe. Despite their criticisms and even mockery of the litigious culture of the United States, the Europeans are following the same path. As the European Union evolves, life in Europe will become more and more like life in the United States in the sense that Europeans will increasingly rely on the law and formal rules to regulate their relationships.

Globalization, Capitalism, and Democracy

Humans tend to see the world from the prism of their own cultures, and researchers and writers are no exceptions. Only a small number of thinkers manage to escape this restriction in any age. The general tendency is to accept "our history" as the "normal" or "true" history, and expect that everyone else will have the same experiences and follow essentially the same paths. Because in the United States capitalism and democracy developed hand in hand, it has been assumed by American thinkers in particular that this is the "norm" and all other countries will "progress" along the same path.

An underlying assumption has been that democracy will evolve hand in hand with economic development. Free-market capitalism will lead to improved standards of living. Once per capita income reaches a certain level, typically thought of as around $8,000 (in 2000 prices), then a large enough middle class will have emerged to have an impact on national politics. This growing middle class will consist of engineers, lawyers, medical doctors, teachers, and other university-educated professionals—people with the knowledge and motivation to participate in the political process and change both the way politics is conducted and the outcome of political practices. The result will be greater political participation by a larger segment of the population leading to stronger and stronger democratic trends and eventually democratic institutions.

The idea that a large middle class will both create and preserve democracy is intuitively appealing. After all, in addition to their economic clout, the middle-class professionals are well educated, worldly, and knowledgeable—they would not want to be governed by a dictator, or to live in a politically closed system. The middle class would serve as a kind of buffer between the working class and the rich, bringing to bear a moderating influence so that the poorest group suffers less exploitation, but at the same time there is not a radical revolt against the rich and the overthrow of the entire political system.

But practical experience has proven that the growth of democracy and free-market capitalism do not necessarily go hand in hand. Indeed, the American experience may well be the exception rather than the rule. In case after case concerning different countries around the world, the twenty-first century has provided examples of growth in a free-market economy, with the emergence of a substantial middle class, without democracy seriously taking root.

Mistaking the Link between Open Economy and Open Society

An open economy does not mean an open society, the largest and most important example being communist China. The Chinese economy has maintained a blistering growth rate of at least 10 percent per annum since the last decade of the twentieth century and is destined to overtake the United States and become the largest economy in the world by the end of the third decade of the this century. The Chinese middle class now numbers several hundred million, and higher education is very rapidly expanding in China with a new focus on research and development intended to add "invented in China" to "made in China" as a label on products sold throughout the world. Chinese business, professional, and academic groups increasingly travel to other countries and are becoming "worldly" both in their knowledge of the world and their consumer tastes.[25] Economically and professionally, China is fairly open, but politically China remains definitely shut. The Chinese communist party maintains a very firm grip on power and there are no indications of this situation seriously changing any time soon.

In addition to the uniquely important case of China, there are numerous other examples of smaller countries in South America, the Caucuses, and other regions of Asia showing that economic growth and movement toward a free-market economy does not necessarily correspond with growth in democracy. Of course, Russia is another important example where the economy has opened up far more than has the political system since the fall of the Soviet empire in 1989. There is a new rich elite in Russia along with a fast growing, consumer-oriented middle class, but the reigns of political power are firmly in the hands of a very small number of men.[26] Indeed, from the time of the Tzar and the pre-1917 era, one could argue that the tradition of one strong leader ruling over Russia with an iron fist has not really changed. In essence, the Russian dictatorship continues, with very little opportunity for freedom of expression and the development of serious opposition organizations to compete against the ruling elite.

Of course, supporters of the thesis that free-market growth and democracy go hand in hand can always argue that their thesis will be proven correct in the long term. "Just wait a few more decades, and the free-market economy and the growth of a new middle class is sure to lead to a democracy," they might claim. But this kind of "just wait, we will prove correct in the long term" approach obviously should not be taken seriously; it fails to meet the falsifiability criterion highlighted by Karl Popper as essential for a scientific hypothesis.

CONCLUDING COMMENT

Globalization as it is actually taking place, what I have termed fractured globalization, is associated with gigantic contradictions and challenges, and is resulting in major problems around the world. Part of why we are not taking up the challenge of dealing with these problems in a correct manner is because we do not really understand the enormity of the changes underway. We see the tip of the iceberg, but the massive impact of fractured globalization remains hidden underneath the surface of the water.

We need to think back to other trans formational periods in history and remind ourselves of the size of the problems that arose. For example, the first industrial revolution created enormous wealth and productivity in the eighteenth and nineteenth centuries, but also huge disparities in living conditions. The millions of peasants who migrated from rural to new urban centers found themselves living and working in grim industrial slums. Governments were slow to regulate the new industries and the slums that swelled up around factories, as young children joined adults in working barbarically long hours in hellish new industrial conditions. It took the latter part of the nineteenth century and most of the twentieth century for government reforms to deal with the excesses of the industrial revolution in western societies.

In the midst of the industrial revolution, irrational and destructive reactions arose against industrialization. For example, in the period 1812–1816 the Luddites, named after a labor leader named Ned Ludd, engaged in machine breaking and sabotaging as a strategy to try to improve the wages and conditions of working people.[27] This was an emotion-based reaction to perceived threat, a threat that we dismiss in hindsight but which people did not fully understand but took very seriously at the time. Fractured globalization will result in far more radical and widespread reactions, from radical environmentalism to Islamic terrorism.

We have only just started to experience the impact of fractured globalization. We can better understand this impact by considering the larger evolutionary context of recent changes, and this we do in the next chapter.

PART TWO

Catastrophic Evolution and Terrorism

Memories of my childhood tumbled out as I rode high on the red double-decker London bus. I had lived in London with my family and used to ride in such buses frequently. The bus was winding past Little Venice, near my old neighborhood, and everything seemed so familiar; the sights and smells took me back to my childhood world. Yet, although I could not put my finger on it at first, it was clear that something about the surroundings had changed dramatically—the voices on the bus were very different. I could now hear Spanish, Polish, French, Russian, Arabic, Urdu, and some other languages I could not recognize. And, yes, I could also hear English being spoken on the London bus. Europeanization is in full swing.[1]

"So few English people left in London now," commented an elderly English lady sitting next to me on the bus. "Lets face it," she added with a wink in her eye, "even the government is foreign. I don't know what's worse, Scottish prime ministers or Polish plumbers."

My smile seemed to encourage her and she added, "Look at this bus, we have a mini United Nations right here."

Enormous migrations are transforming western societies at the turn of the twenty-first century, but they are also changing patterns of contacts between groups all around the world. In Chapter 6, I explore the consequences of these "sudden" intergroup contacts, giving particular importance to the speed at which changes are taking place and groups are being brought face to face. Looking at the contemporary situation from an evolutionary perspective, I argue that sudden contact between groups can under certain conditions result in the demise and even extinction of one or both groups. But such demise or extinction does not come about without reactions and the triggering of defense mechanisms, some of which are dysfunctional. Terrorism is an example of a dysfunctional defense mechanism intended to enhance group survival.

I shall explore in greater detail two related ways in which Islamic fundamentalists feel particularly threatened as a result of fractured globalization. The first involves identity (discussed in Chapter 7), the second involves rights and duties, which are integral to collective identity particularly (discussed in Chapter 8). Underlying threats related to both identity and rights and duties is the perceived hegemony of the United States and the American values being exported to the Islamic world. Fundamentalists believe that these values are, first, not actually reflected in the policies implemented by the U.S. government and, second, contradictory to pure Islam even when they are implemented. An example of such values are the rights of women, gays, and other minorities.

Importantly, the discussions in the next three chapters seriously question the rational model of human behavior, and directly or indirectly endorse an irrationalist view of humankind. My assumption is that most of the time most people are unaware of the factors that are really influencing their behavior, although people are very good at rationalizing their behavior, particularly after an action has been taken. To give an example using the tragic Iraq war launched by the United States and its allies in 2003, war is waged with the avowed intention of "preventing the spread of weapons of mass destruction," and then when no weapons are found, the justification of war is changed with each passing year, from "spreading democracy" to "preventing terrorism," and so on. Humans are creative in justifying even their most heinous actions, but not in acknowledging their own deeper motives.

This tendency for irrational forces to shape behavior becomes magnified through sudden intergroup contact. According to an intriguing new theory,[2] this is because contact with outsiders reminds us of our own mortality. When we are surrounded by our in-group members, we are sheltered and our mortality does not enter consciousness in a threatening manner. For example, Joe's group believe that they and only they will go to heaven after death, and all others will go to the other place that is not so nice. According to the belief system of Joe's group, the world was made in four days using goat milk and all goes well as long as they interact with other in-group members who share this belief. The four days/goat milk people are happy until they come into contact with Ahmed's people, who firmly believe that the world was made in ten days using camel milk. Ahmed's people claim that their belief system is correct and that they and only they are all going to heaven. The problem is that according to both Joe's and Ahmed's groups, only one of them is correct and only one of them is going to heaven. When the two groups meet, they pose serious threats to one another, resulting in reactions that are sometimes extreme and violent. Fractured globalization is leading to sudden contact between many groups similar to those of Joe and Ahmed.

CHAPTER 6

Intergroup Contact and Catastrophic Evolution

" . . . there is the clearest evidence that a cross between individuals of the same species, which differ to a certain extent, gives vigour and fertility to the offspring; and that close interbreeding continued during several generations between the nearest relations, if these be kept under the same conditions of life, almost always leads to decreased size, weakness, and sterility."

—Charles Darwin[1]

Thousands of years before Charles Darwin (1809–1882) wrote about the benefits of crossbreeding and the detrimental effects of inbreeding, these ideas had been put into practice. Farmers and shepherds had learned that by selectively introducing "new blood" into a stock of their domesticated animals, bringing about "intergroup contact," they could change and often improve the characteristics of these animals. The result would be faster horses, dogs with keener senses, chickens that are more hardy in the face of disease, cows able to give more milk, and other changes that can make animals more useful to humans in carrying out their daily tasks and surviving.

By introducing "new blood" into their stocks, farmers and animal breeders selectively mimic natural trends in the wild. Crossbreeding takes place continuously under natural conditions among wild animals as the members of one group roam into the territory of other groups and as migrations bring together enormous numbers of animals from different groups. The evolutionary benefits of such behavior patterns were clear to Darwin and others well before the pioneering research of Gregor Mendel

(1822–1884) became recognized and the genetic mechanisms underlying the consequences of crossbreeding were discovered. Of course, the basics of these mechanisms are common to all life forms, not just animals.

But although crossbreeding among animals and plants can have beneficial results, intergroup contact between different life forms does not always result in outcomes that are beneficial to both groups. Such contact might result in no change to the survival chances of either group, or changes that are beneficial to the survival of both groups, or change that benefits only one of the two groups and detrimentally impacts the other, or changes that detrimentally impacts both groups. The detrimental impact of intergroup contact has been a focus of the environmental movement, as part of a broader concern about global warming and rapid decline in diversity among animals and plants.

Parallel to the debate about the decline in diversity among animals and plants is a second debate about a decline in diversity among human cultures and languages. These two debates have proceeded side by side with very little meaningful communications and crossfertilization: the first, concerning animals and plants, conducted mainly among biologists, ecologists, and various environmental scientists; the second, concerning cultural and linguistic diversity, involving mainly psychologists, linguists, anthropologists, and various other social scientists. This lack of communications between thinkers involved in the two different debates means that very important opportunities are being missed because there are common underlying processes shared by declining diversity among humans and among animals and plants.

CATASTROPHIC EVOLUTION

These common underlying processes are captured by a concept that is the main focus of this chapter: *catastrophic evolution*, a swift, sharp, and often fatal decline in the numbers of a particular life form.[2] Catastrophic evolution can come about through intergroup contact. In this section, I assess the conditions that must be in place for intergroup contact to result in catastrophic evolution, particularly resulting in the near or actual extinction of one of the groups that have come into intergroup contact.

The stepping stone to understanding catastrophic evolution are two related concepts. The first concept is *preadaptiveness*, how "prepared" a life form is in terms of biological and other characteristics for successful evolution in contact with particular other life forms in a given environment. The second concept is *postcontact adaptation speed*, how quickly a life form can adapt, under given environmental conditions, to contact

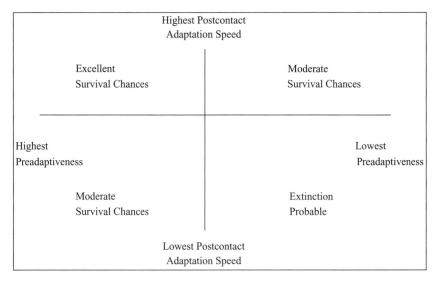

FIGURE 6.1
Diagramatical Representation of Survival Chances under Different Conditions of Preadaptation and Postcontact Adaptation Speed.

with another life form that is in some way or another their competitor in given environmental conditions (of course, if conditions change, they might no longer be competitors).

The alternatives presented by preadaptiveness and postcontact adaptation speed can be conceived as lying at some point in a space delimited by two vectors (see Figure 6.1). The first vector has "highest preadaptiveness" at one extreme of the continuum and "lowest preadaptiveness" at the other extreme. High preadaptiveness means that a life form (in contact with particular other life forms and in a given environment) has a high probability of survival, whereas low preadaptiveness means that a life form under the same conditions has low probability of survival. The second vector has "highest postcontact adaptation speed" at one extreme and "lowest postcontact adaptation speed" at the other extreme. High postcontact adaptation speed means that a life form will be able to increase in numbers while interacting with a particular other life form under given environmental conditions, low postcontact adaptation speed means that a life form will decrease in numbers or even become extinct while interacting with a particular other life form under given environmental conditions.

Catastrophic evolution proposes that a life form with low preadaptiveness and low postcontact adaptation speed will have very low survival chances when it encounters a competitor through *sudden contact*, the swift coming together of life forms with no previous history of contact. Life forms with high preadaptiveness and high postcontact adaptation speed have a very good chance of surviving and thriving after sudden contact. Sudden contact can come about through natural processes, but it can also come about through human influence and direct intervention. The extinction of numerous plants and animals particularly over the course of last century, and the associated rapid decline in biodiversity, have come about in large part through human activities (a topic I discuss later in this chapter).

THE CONTACT HYPOTHESIS AND SUDDEN CONTACT

Over half a century ago the American psychologist Gordon Allport proposed that increased contact between two groups would lead to improved relationships between the groups, but only if certain conditions are met (Allport's research was introduced in Chapter 4). Hundreds of studies have examined the preconditions for successful contact. Until recently, although there was not a general agreement about which particular preconditions are necessary for intergroup contact to lead to improved intergroup relationships, there was agreement that some preconditions are necessary. To sum up in the words of two leading researchers "Contact is not enough."[3] But other researchers who have reviewed all the research on the contact hypothesis suggest that contact can be enough.[4] How do we resolve this disagreement?

Obviously, if we consider examples such as contact between Tasmanians and western settlers, contact was not enough to lead to improved intergroup relations because it resulted in the annihilation of Tasmanians in the nineteenth century. So we necessarily return to the question that contact under what conditions will result in improved intergroup relations? Although numerous researchers have addressed this question and some fascinating solutions have been proposed, a key weakness has been that researchers have failed to consider contact over long enough time periods. This is perhaps not surprising, given that the research methods used by social scientists studying contact, methods such as the laboratory experiment, the questionnaire, and the interview, involve about 60–90 minutes of time spent with each participant. In contrast, the consequences of intergroup contact often take many years—decades and centuries in some cases—to manifest themselves.

According to catastrophic evolution theory, the long-term consequences of sudden contact depend on the adaptiveness of the groups in contact. Higher adaptiveness means greater likelihood of survival. Of course, adaptiveness depends largely on the characteristics of the environment and the out-group involved in the interaction. For example, an in-group can have high adaptiveness in environment E1 when in contact with out-group O1, but low adaptiveness in environment E1 when in contact with group O2.

Factors Shaping Level of Adaptiveness

The key factors that determine the level of adaptiveness are usefully conceptualized as being of two types:

1. Factors that help defend the group:
   - *Size*: The larger the size of a group, the better it will be able to survive aggressive contact.
   - *Military power*: The stronger a group is militarily, the less likely it will become the target of aggressive contact and, if it does become a target, the better it will be able to survive aggressive contact.
   - *Belief system*: Certain belief systems (including religions) help groups to resist aggressive contact and enhance group survival. The effectiveness of belief systems in this task depends in large part on the characteristics of the invading competitor.
2. Factors that attract competitors to launch aggressive contact:
   - *Territory*: Groups who occupy larger territories are more likely to attract aggressive contact by competitors.
   - *Minerals and other material resources*: Groups who occupy territory that is richer in natural resources (such as oil) are more likely to attract aggressive contact by competitors.
   - *Human labor*: The availability of human labor that can be enslaved or put to work at a low price is more likely to attract aggressive contact by competitors.

Thus, a first set of factors protect a group and a second set of factors make it more likely that a group would be attacked.

My argument, then, is that under certain conditions, intergroup contact between life forms can result in catastrophic evolution and the extinction of one or even both of the life forms. Second, that in order to protect themselves and prevent their extinction, life forms develop defense mechanisms, some of which are more adaptive than others (depending on environmental conditions). Radicalization and terrorism are best understood in this evolutionary context as examples of defense mechanisms adopted by human groups that feel threatened with extinction. Of course, the fact that a defense mechanism is adopted does not mean that it is adaptive and will succeed in preventing a sharp decline or even extinction of a group.

Carriers and the Limits of Genetic Explanations

Let me emphasize that I am not proposing a genetic explanation for why terrorism is adopted as a group defense mechanism. The results of the Human Genome Project have made clear that in terms of numbers, the difference between humans and other living creatures, such as fruitfly and mice, is a matter of just a few hundred genes. Most of our approximately twenty-five thousand protein-coding genes in the human genome are shared by some other living creatures.[5] The implication is that the influence of genes on human thought and action, and on human collective behavior, comes about through very complex interactions between genes and the environment. While some researchers have been quick to (mistakenly) jump at simplistic genetic explanations of human thought and action and emphasized the biological basis of human evolution, there has been far too little emphasis on cultural evolution and the transmission of practices associated with human thought and action across long evolutionary periods.

Continuities in human thought and action are in large part made possible through cultural carriers (discussed in Chapter 1 of this book), which serve as hooks on which communities hang values, norms, and other features of their cultures. The veil worn by women in Islamic communities is an example of a sacred carrier. Like a national flag, the veil is just a piece of cloth, but just as a national flag takes on enormous significance and becomes something sacred to defend and even die for, the veil serves as a marker for group identity and something to be defended at all costs. Through carriers and the role they play across generations, communities are able to perpetuate their particular ways of doing and thinking.

The significance of carriers becomes even greater during intergroup contact, when an in-group encounters an out-group that seems threatening. For example, consider contact between secular western groups and fundamentalist Muslims who strongly believe that the survival of their community is jeopardized if women born as Muslims stop wearing the veil. The attraction of secular western culture, with its promise of individual freedom, personal choice, gender equality, and its various exciting features from the perspective of youth, immediately becomes a challenge for fundamentalist Muslims (as it is a challenge for minority religious groups in the West, such as the traditional Amish in the United States). In order to better understand this perceived threat and the reactions it leads to on the part of fundamentalist Muslims, it is useful to step back and consider the macro-evolutionary context of intergroup contact. This topic is first considered in relation to animals and plants and then in relation to human groups.

BIODIVERSITY AND CATASTROPHIC EVOLUTION

There is growing awareness that biological diversity is markedly in decline, and that the rate of species extinction, already about one every twenty minutes, continues to increase. The decline in biological diversity is undoubtedly a result of human activities, associated with deforestation, environmental pollution, and overuse of natural resources by rapidly growing human populations. Together with the impact of global warming, these changes are placing considerable stress on the natural environment. I am writing this chapter in Australia, a vast continent with enormous natural resources and a population that has not yet risen above 22 million. However, even here in the vast spaces of Australia, the strain placed on the natural environment by human activities is leading to serious bottlenecks and difficulties, an example being water shortage in major cities like Sydney and Melbourne. The Australian capital, Canberra, represents an example of very poor planning and misuse of natural resources. Canberra's design spreads the city's population thinly over a vast area so that utilities have to be stretched long distances and everyone has to rely on automobiles for transportation because it is not economically viable to provide public transportation over such long distances for a thinly and widely dispersed population.

The global pressure on natural resources is also increasing as a result of the "new consumers," the rapidly growing group of people in developing countries, particularly the Asian giants China and India (with a population of over 1 billion each), who are now sufficiently affluent to pursue the western middle-class dream of conspicuous consumption. Even though (as we saw at the beginning of this chapter) over half of the developing world's population still live on less that $2 a day, there will soon be an additional billion people in the developing world who can now afford the western middle-class lifestyle, including cars and houses with televisions, washing machines, dishwashers, air conditioners, and other high-energy use consumer goods (the largest groups of new consumers are in China, India, Russia, Brazil, and Mexico). In their analysis of the new consumers, Meyers and Kent note that at the start of the twenty-first century the biggest consumer boom is not taking place in the West "... but in certain developing and transition countries where over 1 billion people now possess the financial muscle to enjoy a consumerist lifestyle."[6] The result is dramatically increased utilization of natural resources and increased environmental degradation and further decline in biological diversity.

Of course, it is highly beneficial that more people in the developing world are enjoying a higher standard of living. However, it is not beneficial that the new consumers of the developing world are emulating the same environmentally destructive lifestyle habits as followed by consumers in the industrialized societies. The best solution, undoubtedly, is for consumers in both western and non-western societies to change their lifestyles to be more environment friendly and supportive of biological diversity.

There is now fairly widespread agreement that a decline in biological diversity should be of serious concern to all humankind. Countless substances useful in human medicine and industries are derived from animals and plants. A decline in the diversity of animal and plant life means that there will be a narrower variety of resources to draw from, and by necessity many potential solutions to challenges confronting humankind in the future will no longer be available. With changing environmental conditions, we shall be facing new challenges that we are not able to predict at present. Many of the solutions that we might have applied to these unforeseen challenges have already become unavailable because the animals and plants that were the source of these solutions are now extinct, and many more such solutions are becoming unavailable because of the threat of extinction confronting many more animals and plants.

Human Activities and Sudden Contact

Animals and plants can come into sudden contact with their competitors through natural processes, resulting in a decline or even extinction of one of the life forms involved in the interaction. However, human activities have dramatically increased the occurrence of sudden contact. Of course, the transportation of animals and plants by humans from one location to another, resulting in sudden contact, is not new. Advances in genetic science has enabled researchers to track, through the Y-chromosomes lineages, the migration patters of early humans out of Africa.[7] This research demonstrates that by around 10,000 years ago all of the major land masses had been reached by human beings. As humans migrated, they slowly contributed to the movement of some types of animals and plants, a process that continued over the last millennium.[8] For example, Maori settlers in the thirteenth century and European settlers in the eighteenth century brought with them many mammals not native to New Zealand, and thirty-five of these mammals quickly adapted and thrived in their new environment.

The rapid adaptation of transported animals and plants is a new focus of evolutionary research; classic Darwinian theory focused more on slow adaptation speed over long-time periods. We now know that under certain conditions some animals and plants can adapt very rapidly and thrive. Consider, for example, the brown tree snake that was accidentally transported to Guam, probably on military cargo planes in the immediate post-World War II period.[9] Because the brown tree snake has no natural predators and a lot of available food in Guam, it has thrived. By the 1990s, the brown tree snake had become extremely numerous (enough to create serious problems for local human inhabitants) and managed to decimate nine out of thirteen of Guam's native forest birds.

The challenges created by invasive species are becoming increasingly serious, as more and more people, goods, and services are transported from place to place around the world. Associated with this global movement of people, goods and services is the transportation of animals and plants—transportation that sometimes takes place by accident and has detrimental consequences. Indeed, problems created by invasive species often come about purely by accident, or at least without intentional malice on the part of people responsible for introducing an invasive species to a new environment. For example, rubber vines, exotic fish and various types of reptiles, as well as countless other types of animals and plants have been "released" into the "wild" (thrown into woods, rivers, and lakes) by owners who did not have "the heart" to kill their pet plants and animals, but found it too difficult to maintain them in the space available in their homes. Once released into a new environment, some of these animals and plants have immediately died, but some others have thrived and proceeded to wipe out many indigenous species, wrecking the local ecological balance.[10]

Thus, sudden contact between different types of animals and plants have been coming about through human activities, resulting in the decline and extinction of some species, and a decrease in biological diversity. Next, I turn to examine sudden contact as it takes place among human groups. Of course, there are major differences between human groups in contact and animals and plants in contact. For example, human groups can become aware of the dangers posed by out-group competitors as well as the threat of sudden contact. This awareness can lead to the intentional development of defense mechanisms as part of efforts to prevent in-group decline and extinction.

HUMAN CULTURAL AND LINGUISTIC DIVERSITY AND CATASTROPHIC EVOLUTION

There is an eerie similarity to the feelings one gets when stepping into museums in the United States, Canada, and Australia, and viewing displays of the cultures of native peoples in these immigrant-receiving countries. I experienced it once again today, when I went to the Australian Museum in downtown Sydney, the sad feeling one gets when observing disappearing civilizations. Of course, the aboriginal people of Australia are still in existence, as are the native people of Canada and the United States. But the sad fact is that the aboriginal people in Australia, like the native people of Canada and the United States, experienced a sharp decline through sudden contact with western settlers.[11] After sudden contact, the common fate of such native people has been to experience near extinction as distinct cultural and linguistic groups.

Just as we should be concerned about declining diversity among animals and plants, we must concern ourselves with declining diversity among human cultures. As environmental conditions change, humans will face new challenges and will need to discover new solutions. Some of these solutions might be found in the cultures of minority groups that are already extinct or in decline and in danger of extinction. In addition, diversity in human cultures is of value because those individuals who participate in culturally diverse educational programs learn to become better citizens and more effective participants in democracies.

Human cultural diversity evolved out of the very different experiences groups of humans as they gradually emerged out of Africa and settled in different environmental conditions. The different demands of the environment led to different cultural practices among groups of humans. For example, consider human variation on *aggression*, behavior intended to harm others. The Yanomamo are people with a fierce reputation who live in the jungles of northern Brazil and southern Venezuela. Yanomamo males routinely engaged in collective violence, raiding rival villages, harming rival males and stealing women—the kinds of behavior that sociobiologists cite to support their genetic-based explanations.[12] While the Yanomamo are isolated by dense Amazon jungles, the traditional Tiwi of northern Australia were isolated by water—they lived on Melville and Bathurst Islands and had little contact with mainland Australia before 1890.[13] In contrast to the Yanomamo, the Tiwi did not engage in collective violence and developed elaborate social practices to avoid collective conflict.

For example, a common dispute in traditional Tiwi society was between old men who monopolized resources and tended to have numerous wives at the same time (including very young ones), and young men who lacked resources had no wives, and were kept in isolated groups as much as possible. Not surprisingly, despite all the barriers and constraints on young men, sexual affairs would take place between the young wives of old men and young men without wives. An old man suspecting such an elicit affair between one of his wives and a young man would publicly accuse the young man and also have the right to throw spears at the accused, but only from a specified distance (rather like a pitcher hurling balls at a batter, but in this case the pitcher is an old man and the batter is young and agile). As a general rule, the aged spear-thrower would have a tough time hitting the young culprit from the designated distance, and the dispute would end when even a slight wound occurred and blood was drawn. Most importantly, the dispute was resolved at the interpersonal level and was not allowed to escalate to the intergroup level.

Now, imagine what would happen if the Yanomamo, a relatively fierce group accustomed to collective violence, were transported and suddenly placed in northern Australia, in contact with the Tiwi, who are far less aggressive and have no living experience with collective violence. Also, imagine if the Yanomamo are also armed with far more advanced weapons and technology so that the Tiwi are at an insurmountable disadvantage relative to their newly arrived competitors. This is the kind of situation many traditional people found themselves in, when western Europeans suddenly appeared on their doorsteps in different parts of Africa, Asia, Australia, and North America.

Sudden Contact and Rapid Decline

The results of sudden contact between western Europeans and various non-western native people were devastating, resulting in dramatic decline and sometimes even the extinction of entire populations. For example, approximately 5 million or so Native Americans lived in the boundaries of the present United States in the fifteenth century (some estimates put this figure as many times higher[14]), but by 1910 only about 220,000 were left alive.[15] Similar declines in native populations occurred in Africa, where the slave trade took an enormous toll on the native population.[16] The slave trade brutalized millions of Africans directly by enslaving them, but it also had a severe and detrimental impact on Africans left in Africa.

Sudden contact with western Europeans resulted in total destruction for some non-western groups. For example, western Europeans first landed on the island of Tasmania in 1642. Although it was not until the early nineteenth century that large numbers of settlers started to arrive in Tasmania, sudden contact with the local inhabitants resulted in total destruction of the local societies.[17] As settlers pushed inland to "claim" more and more territory and resources, increasing numbers of native Tasmanians were killed, either directly at the hands of settlers or indirectly through the spread of diseases such as measles and smallpox (diseases that were new to native people and against which they had no immunity). By 1876 the "last Tasmanian" had died (although this is disputed by some people claiming to be descendants of a small number of Tasmanians who apparently did not perish).

Even in the twentieth century, there have been case studies of the impact of sudden contact between "Western civilization" and traditional people, resulting in the rapid destruction of the traditional group. For example, Colin Turnbull[18] provided a very moving account of the plight of the *Ik*, a hunting and gathering group who were prevented from continuing their nomadic life because of the imposition of national boundaries as part of the establishment of modern nation states in Africa. The *Ik* became confined to a small area on the Kenya–Uganda border, and as a result their normal social relationships and moral order completely broke down. The end result was social disintegration and collapse of their community. Those familiar with the plight of native people in Canada, Australia, and the United States recognize this as a familiar narrative.

Language Death and Sudden Contact

The most direct and clear way in which to show the impact of sudden contact is to focus on linguistic diversity, which (as discussed in Chapter 4) has been in sharp decline since the beginning of the colonization of America, Asia, and Africa by western Europeans.[19] There were approximately 15,000 languages thriving in human societies at the time Columbus landed on the American continent. This number has been cut to far less than half at the start of the twenty-first century, and most of the 6,000 or so still surviving languages are in serious danger of extinction by the end of the twenty-first century.

Since the start of the colonial era, an increasing number of human societies are using fewer and fewer languages. Of the almost seven billion humans living today, the majority use just ten languages (Mandarin Chinese is the most commonly used with 1 million speakers and English is the next most commonly used with 600 million speakers). Hundreds of languages only have a few or just one speaker left alive, and it is estimated that by the end of the twenty-second century only about 200 languages are likely to be left.[20] At least several languages are being lost with every passing month.

The fact that the United States followed Great Britain as the most powerful imperial force on earth has meant that English is endorsed as the "official" language of business, diplomacy, and science. This is the first time in human history that one world superpower (Great Britain) has been succeeded immediately by another (the United States) using the same language. The result is that elites throughout the world communicate with one another predominantly in English and aspiring elites in countries as varied as China, Russia, India, France, and Brazil have to learn to function in English. The consequences are increased pressures on local languages, which get pushed aside as trade, politics, and education become more global.

Language death is important because it directly impacts in the chances of group survival. On the one hand, language serves to sustain a world view and a culture that is characteristic of a distinct group. For example, the French language sustains the world view and culture of French people. The exquisite subtleties of French cuisine, wit, and so on, are best captured by the French language. On the other hand, the collective identity of French people is sustained by the French language, which helps to define the boundaries of the French as a group. Numerous historical examples, such as native peoples in North America, show that when a group experiences a loss of language, there is more likely to follow a loss of collective identity. As we shall see in the next chapter, a loss of collective identity can have a serious, detrimental impact on personal identity.

Of course, the fact that English and a few other languages are becoming global does not mean that the same "English language" is spoken everywhere. Over the last few months I have traveled in the United States, the United Kingdom, Canada, and Australia, and even a comparison between these "Western" societies shows some differences in the way people speak English. A comparison of English-language usage across India, Scotland, Hong Kong, and some other societies would show even more substantial differences in the use of the English language. So, in this sense there are multiple "Englishes," as there are multiple "Spanishes," and so on. But although this point about diverse use of a particular language is relevant, it does not negate the fact of language death and the decline in linguistic diversity more broadly.

The same trend is taking place in the area of religious diversity. Colonialism and imperialism has led to Christianity and some other major religions spreading around the world, and associated with this trend is a decline in local, smaller religions. Of course, it could be argued that there are many, many Christianities, and that local people practice a major religion such as Catholicism in their own "different" ways. Thus, the Hispanics in South America (and also in the United States) practice Catholicism in ways that are different from the ways Catholicism is practiced in Rome. Similarly, Anglicans in Africa practice their version of Christianity in ways that are different from Anglicans in the United Kingdom (for example, African Protestants have shown themselves to be far more traditional on issues such as gay marriage and female priests). Despite the validity of this point, it does not negate the fact that overall religious diversity has been declining.

CONCLUDING COMMENT

A bomb explosion, shredded bodies, blood in the air . . . the immediate horror of terrorist attacks pull us into instinctive reactions and short-term thinking. Unfortunately, the leading politicians of the United States and other western societies have also tended to encourage short-term thinking and "instant counter-attacks" to combat terrorism. Political eyes have remained fixed on the next election, rather than on the "big picture." We need to think beyond the next election cycle and to move toward ending terrorism through long-term concepts and plans.

The theory of catastrophic evolution demands that we consider terrorism in the context of large-scale evolutionary processes. Terrorism is one type of reaction, albeit a dysfunction one, to sudden contact and the threat of extinction. Sudden contact has been accelerated through fractured globalization, and it is likely that this process will continue through the twenty-first century. Islamic fundamentalists are one of a number of groups that perceive themselves to be in danger of decline and extinction, and this "danger" is particularly associated with identity, the topic of the next chapter.

CHAPTER 7

Threatened Identities, Change, and Globalization

The West "needs an enemy, and this time it is Islam," Khatami said. "And Islamophobia becomes a part of all policies of the great powers, of heg[e]monic powers."
    —Former Iranian President Mohammad Khatami[1]

"No Muslim will ever ignore these acts of blasphemy."
    —Pakistani Prime Minister Shaukat Aziz, referring to cartoons, satirizing the Prophet Mohammad, published in Western media[2]

"Muslim children in this country tend to live separate lives... Whether they go to Muslim school does not make much difference to their segregation. They are concentrated in the inner cities. They could be attending a state school that is 90 percent Muslim..."
    —Professor Mark Halstead, describing the education of Muslim children in the United Kingdom[3]

Complex political, economic, social, and psychological factors have combined to create circumstances in which Muslim communities in both western and non-western countries, and practicing Muslims in particular, fundamentalist Muslims even more so, feel collectively threatened. This perceived threat is a distressing psychological experience, associated with feelings of collective shame, frustration, and anxiety. Among Muslims in the West, practicing and fundamentalist Muslims tend to be segregated and have developed self-protective mechanisms against prejudice, akin to the ways in which African-Americans and other minorities have protected their self-esteem in ethnic enclaves in western societies.[4] By looking inward, Muslims in both western and non-western societies are able to collaboratively construct and collectively support a social reality that is in harmony with a positive view of themselves. However, when they look outward and when they interact with the mainstream western world, as they must in order to survive and succeed in the larger world, Muslims are forced to face a far more hostile and threatening world.

SOURCES OF THREATS TO ISLAMIC IDENTITY

The source of this threat is often described by Muslims as being western powers, and the United States and Israel in particular. At the heart of this threat is seen to be the interests of Zionism and American Imperialism, which are seen to coincide and to work against Muslim interests. The Israeli lobby in Washington, DC, is seen to be exerting considerable influence over decisions made by the U.S. government. Of course, Muslims are not alone in claiming that the Israeli lobby in Washington, DC is exerting undue influence; this view is shared by a number of different factions in western societies. A best-selling book by John Mearsheimer and Stephen Walt,[5] university professors at Chicago and Harvard respectively, has presented arguments in support of the same claim. But whereas Mearsheimer and Walt attempt to analyze the influence of the Israeli lobby objectively, the assessments that many Muslims make of the situation are strongly linked with deep emotions and feelings of threats against their in-group. Tragically, the real potential for Muslim societies to gain from the democratic and open traditions of Israeli society remains untapped. Again and again, despotic rulers in Muslim countries manage to use "the Israeli threat" as an excuse to stamp out democratic movements within Muslim societies.

This feeling of threat has been intensified by television and other media coverage showing Muslims under military attack in Palestine, Iraq, Afghanistan, and Lebanon, among other places. Gruesome images of Muslim civilians, including women and children, being killed by American high-tech weapons, has inflamed anti-American feelings and radicalized at least some, typically younger groups of Muslims, even in western societies. The social isolation of millions of South Asian Muslims in the United Kingdom, North African Muslims in France, Turkish Muslims in Germany, and other groups of Muslims experiencing segregation in the rest of Europe, has heightened this perceived threat.

Between the terrorist attacks of 9/11 in the United States and the plot foiled in August 2007 to commit terrorist attacks in Germany, there were far more actual and planned terrorist attacks in Europe than in North America. The attacks in Europe include the March 11, 2004, train bombings in Spain (killing almost 200 people), the July 7, 2005, suicide bombings on the London transit system (killing 52 people), the June 2007 attack at Glasgow airport, and failed bombing attack in London. Among the foiled terrorist plots, the public knows of attempts by would-be attackers to bomb the London Underground (subway) in July 2005, to bomb commuter trains in Cologne, Germany in July 2006, and to blow up passenger planes going from the United Kingdom to the United States in August 2006. In September 2006 and 2007, groups of Muslim men were arrested in Denmark on suspicion of making bombs to be used in terror attacks. These actual and foiled terror attacks underline the point that Muslim communities in Europe are facing major integration challenges. In order to better understand the relationship between Muslims and their out-groups, we need to look closely at broad, global, and evolutionary trends.

In my analysis of the experiences and perceptions of Muslim communities, I give particular attention to macro-level globalization trends and long-term evolutionary processes. The threat perceived by traditional Muslims needs to be understood in the context of globalization, sudden increased intergroup contact, massive movements of populations, and evolutionary changes often associated with the demise and even extinction of minority cultures and languages. Such transformations are not shaped by moral, ethical, or normative criteria, but by functionality.

I begin by examining identity needs, one of the most important examples of human psychological universals (discussed in Chapter 3). Related to identity needs is another important human universal (also discussed in Chapter 2), the need for a minimum level of control. Globalization seriously threatens both of these needs for large segments of the human population. Practicing and fundamentalist Muslims feel this threat particularly acutely. But in order to understand this perceived threat in more depth, we must get at the heart of globalization changes and identify what about these changes is particularly threatening some groups. Thus, in the second major part of the chapter, I discuss the puzzle of globalization changes. Finally, in part three the focus is on the frightening feeling of "declining or lost control" that raises anxiety and frustration among many Muslims.

A FUNCTIONAL VIEW OF IDENTITY NEEDS

Observant travelers who journey to Muslim communities, both in western and non-western societies, inevitably become aware of the acute focus on identity and threats to their collective identity among Muslims in the twenty-first century. I have gone as far as to argue that the Islamic world is experiencing a collective identity crisis.[6] By which I mean Muslim communities are seriously troubled by answers they find to questions such as:

What kind of people are Muslims?
What kind of people do we want to become?
Are Muslims valued in the larger world?

Received wisdom tells us that the really important factors are material resources, such as land, oil, and water. Compared to the "hard," more important factors of material resources, issues of identity are "soft," "divorced from the practical world," and in some ways unimportant in terms of the "nuts and bolts of real life." However, I argue that the issue of collective identity is of the highest practical importance and absolutely crucial to the long-term survival chances of a group. People can have land, oil, and water, but still suffer inadequate collective identity.

There are two reasons in particular as to why the collective identity crisis of Muslim communities, a crisis that has been brewing over the last century, has reached a climax at the start of the twenty-first century. The first is the perceived military assault on the Muslim world, most recently as represented by the invasion of Iraq by the U.S.-led forces in 2003. The impact of this invasion and its aftermath has not been fully recognized by the western mainstream. Even the many western critics of the war, which includes the majority of people in the United States, its "war ally" the United Kingdom, and other major western societies, have neglected an important issue: how the 2003 invasion has made Muslim communities in both western and non-western countries feel utterly vulnerable and weak.

The U.S.-led forces smashed into Iraq in 2003, swept aside the central government and the ruling elite in Baghdad, and then completely failed to manage the situation to bring about peace, security, and progress. There ensued a breakdown of law and order, devastating sectarian violence, leading to millions of Iraqi refugees, and the deaths of hundreds of thousands of Iraqi civilians. Since 2003, life for ordinary Iraqis in Baghdad and a number of other major population centers has been characterized by insecurity, lower living standards, and less reliable services such as electricity. The only major region to experience progress since the 2003 invasion is Kurdistan in the north of Iraq. Even with the so-called "surge" in troops and the change in the patterns of violence in Iraq in 2007 and 2008, so much damage has been inflicted there by successive wars since the later 1970s that it will take at least another generation to improve living conditions in Iraq to an acceptable level.

The 2003 invasion of Iraq has brought about an intense sense of collective insecurity to people in Muslim societies, particularly in the Near and Middle East and in North Africa. Day after day of seeing images of death and destruction in Iraq, year after year of turmoil and insecurity, have brought home a vital message: this could happen to us! America could invade our country! This heightened anxiety and intense feeling of collective insecurity have been partly shaped by the rhetoric comings from the George W. Bush White House: "You are with us or against us," "good versus evil," and so on. From the perspective of Muslim populations, President Bush sees Muslims as the evil enemy.

How can people in Muslim communities protect themselves and prevent what happened in Iraq happening to them? How can they protect themselves and their families? What is to prevent American bombs from falling on their cities, American troops from trampling through their homes? What can stop the horrific events of Abu Ghraib being repeated in their societies?

However, we should not imagine that this perceived threat has evaporated when George W. Bush has left the White House at the end of his eight-year term as U.S. President. Images of what happened in Abu Gharib prison are seared into the collective memory of Muslims around the world. These images are part of the collective consciousness of Muslim communities everywhere, and are integral to the feelings of collective shame and insecurity experienced by Muslims. Abu Gharib images have become the flashbulb memories that bind Muslims together, giving them continued reasons to feel insecure.

It is with this collective insecurity in mind that we must interpret the success of Muslim political movements in major Islamic societies, including Turkey and a number of other countries that previously seemed "safely secular." From the perspective of the Muslim world, Iraq has been brutalized by U.S.-led forces—under the pretext of "weapons of mass destruction," which turned out to be nonexistent in Iraq. How can Muslim communities protect themselves? In the face of the rape of Iraq, Muslim people have circled the wagons to become more defensive and more rooted to Islam. Thus it is that Turkey, a "traditionally secular country" of the modern world has democratically elected an Islamic leaning group to power.

Demographics and Identity in the Islamic World

A second major factor contributing to the "crisis of identity" in Islamic communities arises from the demographic characteristics of Muslim populations. The Muslim societies with the largest populations (2008 figures) include Indonesia (250 million), Pakistan (155 million), Bangladesh (140 million), Nigeria (135 million), and Iran and Turkey (both with approximately 75 million each). A number of other Muslim countries have enormous territories and mineral resources, but relatively small populations (e.g., Kazakhstan, with a territory equivalent to all of western Europe, only has a population of 16 million, and Saudi Arabia, with the largest known oil reserves of any country, has a population of only 27 million). But the key to Muslim populations is their youth rather than just their present size: approximately 60 percent of the global Muslim population is below the age of 25.

The enormous size of the young sector in the Muslim world means that identity is front and center as a societal issue for Muslims around the globe. The importance of identity in the life of the young is underscored in the major theories of human development.[7] For example, in Erik Erikson's (1902–1994) eight-stage model of lifelong development, the main developmental challenge at the stage of adolescence is to move from childhood to adulthood by evolving a healthy, clear sense of identity. It is the young who are more likely to question the nature and adequacy of the group identity, in part because they are experiencing change most dramatically and attempting to find their own place in a changing world.

Those individuals who fail in the challenge to develop a healthy identity and experience what Erikson refers to as role confusion rather than a healthy identity, face enormous challenges as adults and are more likely to be psychologically and socially dysfunctional. But the essential feature of such dysfunction is that it does not arise from the purely private experiences of isolated individuals. Rather, identity dysfunction at the personal level is integrally related to identity development at the collective level. This analysis is in line with the approach taken by the Canadian researcher Donald Taylor, who argues that,

> . . . collective identity is rationally and psychologically primary, and therefore is the most important component of the self-concept. For groups that have a well-defined collective identity, attention naturally turns to personal identity and esteem. But when collective identity is compromised in any way, the entire self-concept is jeopardized.[8]

In a similar vain, I have argued that the personal perceptions and understandings individuals develop of others, arise out of the collective perceptions and understandings of their group.[9] Thus, *inter-subjectivity*, how individual X understands individual Y, is shaped by *interobjectivity*, how the in-group of individual X understands the the out-group to which individual Y belongs. For example, if X is a white Christian

American male soldier and Y is an Iraqi Shi'a Muslim, the perception that X has of Y will first and foremost be shaped by how white Christian American male soldiers as a group view Iraqi Shi'a Muslims as a group.

The dominance of collective worldview over individual worldview, of interobjectivity over intersubjectivity, arises because the collective always precedes, shapes, and engulfs the individual. The collective worldview is already present and active when we arrive into this world. We learn about in-groups and out-groups through our participation in collective life. The vast majority of us adopt the worldviews of the societies we grow up in, particularly as this worldview pertains to our own group identity and the group identities of outsiders, those who do not belong to our groups. When we grow up in societies that have ambivalent and even negative views of our own collective identity, this has important repercussions for our personal identity.

Hundreds of millions of young Muslims are growing up in societies where the collective identity of Muslims is in crisis, by which I mean there is a deep, pervasive, and serious questioning of the worth, dignity, and honor of Muslim collective identity. When these young people ask the essential questions, "What kind of a group are Muslims?" and "Is my group valued in the larger world?" they find ambiguous and even negative answers. From the perspective of many people in Islamic communities, the western world, as represented by American leaders in particular, appears to have adopted an "us against them," "good against evil" viewpoint, with Muslims designated as "evil outsiders." Given this negative feedback from the West, which dominates the world militarily and in many ways culturally, how should Muslim youth react?

There are two key elements to the reactions of Muslim youth to the collective identity crisis experienced by Muslim societies. The first element has to do with the experience shared by some Muslim youth that they are becoming "copies" of western ideals. The second element has to do with the sense of not having adequate control of one's own group identity. Both of these are further explored below.

The Good Copy Problem

Muslim youth, like all young people, are particularly influenced by role models. The international media provides them with one set of role models: film stars, sports champions, rock musicians, and pop artists generally. They are bombarded night and day with countless images, sounds, and all kinds of exciting messages, an inescapable deluge, glorifying these role models. The common feature of all these messages is Hollywood, even when the role model in the shape of a musician or a film star, or a sports idol is Muslim and local, the original source of the model is western. The local soccer star in Tehran and Karachi and Cairo and Riyadh and Kuwait, and all the other Muslim societies, is ultimately copying soccer stars in the West, where the first soccer stars came into existence and where the greatest soccer stars continue to shine on the international stage.

The adoption of western role models has been encouraged by a variety of governments in Muslim countries, eager to put up at least the facade of a society open to new ideas and trends. Thus, from the early modernization efforts of Kemal Atatürk (1881–1938) in Turkey, to the most recent attempts to put on a "democratic face" by dictators in Egypt, Saudi Arabia, Kuwait, and elsewhere in the Islamic societies of the Near and Middle East, Islamic leaders have felt the strong pull of the West, and the need to present themselves as up with the times. They have felt that they should at least in some important ways copy the western model. In some cases, this western leaning has been explicit and public, such as in the case of the Shahs of Iran in the twentieth century.

The power of the western role models is clearly evident when we look at the lifestyle of young people in Muslim communities. This is most obvious with respect to fashion, entertainment, electronics, and sport. Global fashion trends are strongly influenced by western fashion centers, particularly New York, London, and Paris. Muslim youth follow these global fashion trends so that underneath her veil a Muslim teenager is likely to be wearing the same style jeans as worn by fashion-conscious American teenager in New York. The cell phones Muslim youth carry around, the music they listen to, the films they watch, the sports teams they follow, even the books they read—these are very often directly from the West. Films such as *Pirates of the Carribean* and books such as the *Harry Potter* series are as popular and well known among Muslim youth as they are among western youth. The global reach of Hollywood advertisers enabled the simultaneous release of the movie *Pirates of the Carribean: At World's End* in over 100 countries in one weekend in 2007.[10] Such enormous reach ensures that no matter how vehemently Islamic fundamentalists preach against the "Great Satan" America, Muslim youth come under the cultural umbrella of the United States.

If you doubt this, travel to a Muslim society in the Near and Middle East and listen to Muslim youth talk about their aspirations and dreams: studying in America, getting a visa to go to America, having the opportunity to live the American Dream... this is what you will hear. Even in the country with the most vehemently anti-American government, the Islamic Republic of Iran, the young will express exactly these sentiments. I was teaching at Tehran University immediately after the revolution of 1978, at a time when anti-Americanism had reached a peak. The hostage-taking crisis was one sign of the atmosphere of that time, when radical students stormed the U.S. embassy in Tehran and took American diplomats as hostages. In the midst of the turmoil and extremist activities, I was asked by one of the student fundamentalists to help her write a letter in English to an American university. I later found out that this vehemently anti-American fundamentalist had relatives in the United States and wanted to join them and to study in America.

This trend of "anti-American" Iranians among the ruling elite in Iran having relatives, bank accounts, and property in the West, and in North America particularly, continues to this day. Some individuals and families involved live extraordinary double lives. They are vehemently anti-American in Iran, but transform into "moderate Muslims" in the West. They do not completely abandon their roots and lives in Iran, because that is where the oil money is, and that is where they have opportunities to "make" large amounts of money through their government connections and the corruption of the system in Tehran. But what allows for this double standard to take place is not just greed and hypocrisy, although that is a large part of it—it is also a deep insecurity about what is Iranian versus what is western. As a general rule, "Western" is taken to mean "better." The ideal model for most things is thought to be western.

Thus, even many of those who express radical Islamic views experience a deep insecurity and are defensive about their identities. It is their insecurity that leads them to reject outgroups so vehemently, particularly powerful outgroups such as the United States that has such an alluring culture. The very attractiveness of American culture for the young in Islamic societies means that American culture has become the most loathed target among radicals.

The modern sector of Islamic societies is particularly influenced by western ideals. Western visitors often remark how Muslim women will arrive at a party wearing a veil and looking traditional, then as soon as they step inside the house and the door to the outside world is closed, they lift their veils and reveal the latest New York fashions.

UNDERSTANDING AND MISUNDERSTANDING CHANGE

According to an ancient proverb, "The eye cannot see the eyelashes," and one could add, "People cannot see the change they are in." We are immersed in continuous change, like fish immersed in flowing water, but it is difficult for us to recognize the movement. What we see are particular episodes and events that stand out, like jagged rocks punctuating the flowing stream.[11]

Changes associated with globalization are especially difficult to recognize, because the body of waters passing through, carrying us along, are humongous and there are so many different currents weaving in and out, bursting forth and disappearing. So, we focus on our own little part of the globalization tsunami. If we are in Miami or New York or London or Paris or Sydney or Berlin, or in some other western center, we tend to focus on job outsourcing to India and China, and the mountains of Chinese products pouring into our local markets, and it is from this particular, narrow, and biased perspective that we evaluate globalization changes. On the other hand, if we are in Cairo or Tehran or Riyadh or Kuwait, or any other center in the Islamic world, our focus is on the cultural floods pouring in, submerging us from the West, bringing millions of seductive voices, singing western values and ideals, waterboarding us in a simulated drowning that seems all too real.

In part because all we humans are living in the midst of globalization changes, it is difficult to understand these changes or even to recognize their immensity. But more broadly, we have never been very good at making sense of change. The modern social sciences, including psychology, sociology, economics, political science, and anthropology, have made very little progress toward explaining change in the human domain. This is partly because change involves so many different levels, from biological and psychological processes inside individuals, to interpersonal relations and processes within groups, to intergroup and macro-societal processes.

Modern specialists have attempted to "divide and conquer" change, to understand change by taking it apart, and this is in some respects a practical strategy. However, "divide and conquer" has not been successful in understanding change because what is also needed is an integrative theory to help put all the parts back together again.[12] The Gestalt motto that, "The whole is more than the sum of its parts" is applicable to change more than it is to any other domain of human life. Once the parts are taken apart, something essential is lost from the whole. Thus, as a consequence of our specialized way of trying to "divide and conquer change," this topic is misunderstood or ignored in the social sciences, it is a topic that falls between the cracks.

Change and Identity

If we attempt to understand change at the abstract level, without bringing it down to concrete events, we are likely to end up grasping nothing of value. But if we restrict our exploration of change to concrete examples, the outcome will be just as sterile. The challenge is to successfully bridge the gap between general, abstract concepts and specific, concrete phenomena. One way to achieve this balance is to consider change in the domain of identity, which is vitally important in the context of globalization, radicalization, and terrorism.

"Globalization will inevitably result in people being all the same," a student critic of globalization complained to me recently, "everyone will end up even looking and sounding the same. Our identities will become so similar, its [sic] scary." From one perspective, the view that globalization will lead to greater and greater similarities seems logical. If the movement toward one "free market" continues, technological and economic forces will result in all of us being in the same commercial market, competing for the same jobs and consuming the same goods. Just as the same fast food outlets (MacDonalds, Pizza Hut, TGIF, and so on) are found around the world, in the future all our goods and services will become global. Irrespective of where we live in the world, we will have the same choices in terms of goods and services.

"People will intermarry so much that we will even end up all looking similar," continued my student, "the world will be filled with like-minded people who look similar, how boring." Yes, globalization is leading to far more movement of populations around the world, from country to country and continent to continent, resulting in much greater contact between the members of different ethnic, linguistic, religious, cultural, and racial groups. But does this change mean increasing intermarriage between groups so that differences between people will "melt away," resulting in "similar looking people" everywhere?

Will globalization result in homogeneity and the end of intergroup differences? Will identities become merged into one? Such change might seem inevitable if we view globalization from the top-down, from the perspective of financial, political, and military elites. For example, in the European context, it is clear that these elites are pushing an agenda to strengthen a unified "European identity." But on the ground floor, on the streets where the majority of people are, changes are not taking place according to this "global" formula.

Macro–Micro Rule of Change

One of the important rules about change is that there are certain limits to how change can be managed in a "top-down" manner. For example, the maximum speed of change at the macro level of economic and political processes is much faster than the maximum speed of change at the micro level of psychological processes. Economic and political elites can instantly bring about changes at the macro level, by changes in governments as well as in political and economic policies. For example, legislation can set up trade barriers or end them, or create unions (such as the European Union) between nations or divide nations and rejoin them (as happened in the case of East and West Germany), and central banks can instantly change the interest rate for borrowing money in a country. But such "top-down" policies are not able to control changes at the psychological level. For example, even after decades of "top-down" policies trying to create a European identity, most people in France, Italy, England, and other members of the European Union still have far stronger ties with their "home countries" than with the European Union. Ask an Englishman or a Frenchman what his loyalty is to, and the answer is more likely to be England or France first, rather than to Europe.[13]

Change is also influenced by "bottom up" processes, by meaning making that takes place involving people in their everyday lives, constructing and sharing, and upholding narratives that give meaning to their activities. People are not passive actors in the face of "top-down" forces influencing them. Rather, people are active in trying to shape events around them, using cultural carriers (discussed in Chapter 1) to preserve and move forward their own interpretations of values and meanings. For example, traditional and fundamentalist Muslims use the Islamic veil (in the case of women) and the beard (in the case of men) as carriers of their values.

THE LOSS OF CONTROL

Globalization involves changes that impact on the sense of control humans experience. However, this impact is not the same for all people in different parts of the world. Just as there are multiple, diverse experiences with globalization around the world, there are many experiences of control in relation to globalization. What is common to human experiences around the world is a sense of loss of control, albeit to different degrees, and a basic need for a minimal level of control (as discussed in Chapter 3).

Loss of Control and Globalization

Of course the North American and European workers who feel threatened by job outsourcing often experience a "loss of control." Of course western consumers who feel that everything they purchase is stamped *Made in China* experience a "loss of control." But in these cases, the perceived threats have to do with jobs and trade.

Chinese goods are seen to be flooding the western markets because they are cheaper, and jobs are being outsourced to India and other societies because labor there is cheaper. The loss of control experienced by westerners through globalization has to do with a sense that cheap labor, goods, and services are taking over the western and world markets. The standard of living of workers in western societies is being threatened.

Similarly, workers in western societies feel threatened because of the growth of Web-based businesses, such as You-Tube and Facebook. These businesses generate enormous revenues for shareholders, but hire very few employees—a couple of hundred employees, compared to the couple of hundred thousand workers employed by some traditional manufacturing companies with similar stock values. Of course, this is a threat to job-seekers, because new technologies seem to have taken control out of the hands of ordinary people. What is the value and bargaining power of labor when so few workers are needed? The decline of traditional manufacturing jobs and the rapid rise of jobs based on electronic communication systems signals less control for the masses and far greater control for a tiny elite. This is *The Winner Takes All Society*[14] run amuck, where a few "winners" take all the spoils and the vast majority of the people are left almost empty handed, competing for low-pay jobs in the global market.

This is very different from a loss of control brought by globalization to non-western societies, and particularly to communities of Muslims around the world. In the case of people in Muslim communities, the loss of control arises from a threat to their culture, values, and identity. One is sharply reminded of this by talking with Muslim parents about their children. Even in Muslim countries that are not in the eye of the Middle East storm, this perceived threat is starkly clear. For example, among the countries I visited last year were Malaysia and Morocco, both Muslim countries "in the periphery" of the Middle East conflict. In Morocco, a conversation I had with an engineer, an employee of an American company based in Morocco, captures the general mood of the parents one meets in such Muslim countries:

"So what is it like working for an American company?" I asked.
Engineer: "I enjoy the technical side of the work, there is always something new to learn. Although the American management is not always very efficient, the technology is wonderful, and for me as an engineer this is something special."
"Would you like more American companies to come to your country?"
"Yes, definitely for my children. They would benefit from a better economy and more job opportunities, that is the up side."
"Is there a down side?"

"Well, more American companies means more American culture being imported here. I am not sure that is always a good thing."

"Why not?"

"Our family lives are very different from American lives, we like to have our children close to us. I don't mean just physically, I mean they should follow our traditions. We don't like our children to live wild lives, we want them to get married with people like us, and have a family too."

"But Americans get married and have families."

"I know, I know, but young people in America are too wild and have too much freedom. They do things the American way. We want our children to follow Muslim practices, but now with all that is coming from America on TV and radio and the Internet and e-mail and You-tube, and magazines . . . it is all too much. We can't keep control of all that is coming here. Our children are being influenced by too many American values."

"Your children must be attracted to these American values."

"They are young, they can't judge, they can't make good decisions. They are seduced by the Hollywood images and the music and the film stars and all the glamorous things coming from America. Young people find it appealing."

"But what is wrong with that?"

"What is wrong is that once we lose control of our own children, once the young in our society turn their backs on their own traditions and families, then our society is lost. We become nothing. We become just producers and consumers of goods."

"So you feel you are losing something?"

"Definitely, we are in danger of losing who we are. The whole world is in danger of becoming lost—no, becoming drowned in American culture."

"Do you think you can stop this?"

"God willing, we will try. I don't want my children to become strangers to me."

"Are they becoming strangers to you?"

"Yes, yes my daughter who is only fifteen secretly collected all kinds of clothes and makeup and started to sneak out of the house without us knowing, to meet other girls and boys who listen to American music and hang around Internet cafes and watch things that we would not allow at home."

"But American parents also complain about their teenage daughters and sons breaking rules and getting into videos and alcohol and all kinds of things forbidden to them."

"That may be, but they are doing this in their own culture. The films and music and alcohol is all part of an American youth culture. When they do it, it is authentic to them. But these things do not belong in our Islamic culture, they are alien to us, they are American imports, like Coca Cola and Pizza Hut and all the millions of other things coming to us from America. These are not our culture, they are American culture."

"Should young people not be free to choose for themselves? If they like American culture, should they not be allowed to have it?"

"No, because then we will be lost. We will give up our own culture and way of life, in the false hope of taking on a better culture and way of life. But this is a false promise. American technology is great, but American culture and values are empty. They result is killing and torture, like in Abu Ghraib."

"A lot of Americans also feel bad about Abu Gharib."

"But that is different. It is like saying a lot of Americans also feel bad about most the Native Peoples in America being wiped out. Yes, they feel bad about it, but they did it. They wiped out those people and put them in reservations. Now the Native People don't have their own cultures any longer, they just dance for tourists. I saw them dance when I visited America."

"So if American culture is so powerful, how can you stop it coming into your society?"

"We also have a strong culture, strong traditions, our Islamic way of life. I want my daughter to live the traditions of Islam, and not copy Western women. Copying the Western culture is our biggest sin."

"Surely globalization is a lot more than Americanization, or even Westernization. What about all the Chinese and Indian and Japanese and Arab and other non-Western influences in your society? Don't they bother you?"

"No, not in the same way as American culture bothers us. The Chinese goods are flooding our markets, and Indian films and music [are] everywhere, and Japanese cars fill our roads...but it is American culture we fear. It is American culture that can suffocate us and steal our children from us."

CONCLUDING COMMENT

The collective identity crisis of Muslim communities, including those in western societies, is influenced by three main factors. The first factor is the immediate military threat posed by the perceived aggression of the United States and its allies, including Israel, as they are seen to push militarily into Muslim lands, such as Iraq and Palestine, and take over Muslim territories. The second factor is the continued rule of alienated dictatorships, such as those in Egypt and Saudi Arabia, that are still in power only because of U.S. support. The third factor, and by far the most important, is the globalization of "American culture," including values and ideals that prove alluring to the younger generation of Muslims. These three factors combined have proven to be a powerful explosive mixture.

The combined impact of this explosive mixture, fermenting in the context of fractured globalization, is leading Islamic fundamentalists to experience anxiety and threat. Perhaps this is to be expected and should be regarded as unavoidable. However, "moderate Muslims" are also feeling threatened and disrespected. Even if we adopt a rationalist approach and rely on surveys of the Islamic world that use explicit straightforward questions, we find that Muslims report that westerners see them negatively and do not have sufficient respect for them.[15] To understand the radicalization and terrorism arising from Muslim communities, I have argued, it is also useful to consider irrational processes that underlie collective threatened identities.

Groups experiencing threats to their collective identities often react in irrational, destructive ways (for example, through terrorist acts), intended to harm others without regard for their own material interests. The goal of such action is not just to inflict pain on the other, but also to humiliate the other (as discussed in Chapter 2). In this way, terrorism and torture are very similar. The deeper goal of both terrorism and torture is to humiliate the other. Just as the American military torturers in Abu Ghraib Prison were intent on humiliating their Iraqi captives, Islamic terrorists in Baghdad are intent on humiliating Americans.

In interviewing Islamic fundamentalists, I have been struck by how often they make remarks such as, "Whatever it costs, we will bring the American government to its knees. We will humble the American government." This intended humiliation of the other arises not from strength, but from threatened collective identity, and a deeper anxiety about becoming extinct. Even the staunchest Islamic fundamentalist can see direction of the global tide, and magnetic pull of American culture for the younger generation. The tragedy of Abu Ghraib is not just that torture took place, but that through creating conditions to bring about torture, Donald Rumsfeld and others in the George W. Bush administration undermined the power and magnetic pull of American culture.

CHAPTER 8

Universal Rights and Duties as Explosive Threats

What is it to be human? There are many ways of answering this question, but in the twenty-first century there is new impetus to provide an answer that includes the idea that all humans have fundamental *rights*, what a person is owed by others—rights are seen as central to the kinds of creatures we humans are, to our identities. For example, if Jane has the right of free speech, then others must provide her with the opportunity to speak freely. On the surface, this would seem to be a noncontroversial issue. Surely, we all agree that all human beings have human rights. Surely the issue of human rights should serve as a rallying cry, a common interest that binds all human groups together to work toward peace? Far from it! In practice, human rights have proved to be a source of intense conflict and an explosive issue associated with major disagreement between groups.

In practice, no other issue seems to demonstrate what Samuel Huntington famously called a "clash of civilizations" as vividly as human rights.[1] Huntington identifies the combination of a number of factors, including western Christianity, the separation of spiritual and temporal authority, the rule of law, social pluralism, and the strength of civil society as contributing in western societies to increased individualism and greater importance being given to individual rights. The absence of the *combination* of these factors in most non-western societies has meant, Huntington argues, that the spread of democracy and human rights did not take place after the collapse of the Soviet Union in 1990, as many had hoped. The West has continued to press in support of democracy and human rights, but "Almost all non-Western civilizations are resistant to this pressure from the West. These include Hindu, Orthodox, African, and in some measure even Latin American countries. The greatest resistance to Western democratization efforts, however, came from Islam and Asia. This resistance was rooted in the broader movements of cultural assertiveness embodied in the Islamic Resurgence and the Asian affirmation."[2]

However, there are also many who oppose the "clash of civilizations" thesis and argue that all humans living in all civilizations inherently have human rights, irrespective of where they live. Received wisdom tells us that the American president George W. Bush and the British Prime Minister Tony Blair were following this line of thinking when they maneuvered to bring about the ill-fated military invasion of Iraq in 2003; the claim is that Bush and Blair were attempting to export democracy and to uphold human rights in *all* societies, including Islamic ones. Bush and Blair apparently believed in globalization and globalized values: all people have the same inherent rights.

But, as I argue below, not everyone agrees that Bush and Blair invaded Iraq with the intention of spreading democracy and supporting human rights. Indeed, many people in the Near and Middle East, as well as in other parts of the world, were influenced by events at Abu Ghraib prison and other places in Iraq, and came to believe that Bush and Blair simply used human rights as an excuse to invade Iraq in order to enjoy better access to Near and Middle East oil and gas reserves. From this alternative, some would say "conspiratorial" perspective, human rights have become a weapon in the hands of western powers intent on robbing non-western societies.

In order to understand how human rights have come to serve as a threat and a source of conflict, rather than a force for peace, we must look to how modern ideas about human rights came into place and to the role of human rights in international relations in the twenty-first century.

HUMAN RIGHTS IN GLOBAL CONTEXT

In the aftermath of the World War II, as the entire world was awakening from a nightmare of destruction and death, the great humanitarian and reformer Eleanor Roosevelt (1882–1962) inspired and cudgeled an international group of representatives gathered in the United States to craft a "universal" list of human rights.[3] This list was developed to eventually become the *Universal Declaration of Human Rights*, adopted by the General Assembly of the United Nations in 1948. In the preamble to the *Universal Declaration of Human Rights*, it states that,

> ... the General Assembly proclaims this Universal Declaration of Human Rights as a common standard of achievement for all peoples and all nations, to the end that every individual and every organ of society, keeping this Declaration constantly in mind, shall strive by teaching and education to promote respect for these rights and freedoms and by progressive measures, national and international, to secure their universal and effective recognition and observance, both among the people of Member States themselves and among the peoples of territories under their jurisdiction.

What could be more natural than all human beings having rights? The *Universal Declaration of Human Rights* contains thirty Articles, each of which spell out certain universal rights, such as "Everyone has the right to life, liberty and security of person" (Article 3) and "No one shall be held in slavery or servitude; slavery and the slave trade shall be prohibited in all their forms" (Article 4). On the surface, at least, these seem non-problematic declarations. Surely the realization of the global village will also mean the acceptance of human rights as a "natural" feature of all societies.

From a western perspective, integral to globalization is the spread of human rights, as human rights are understood by modern international institutions such as the World Court at The Hague (established in 1945 and comprising *The Permanent Court of International Justice* and other courts), and enshrined in the *United Nations Declaration of Human Rights*. Despite the severe criticisms leveled at the United Nations, particularly by right-wing Americans,[4] even critics tend to express support for the *Universal Declaration of Human Rights* (although they are less thrilled when their own countries are accused of violating human rights, as in the case of human rights violations by American and British Military forces in post-2003 invasion in Iraq).

It seems natural that non-western societies should adopt this version of human rights, because it is associated with scientific advances and the much-improved standard of living in the West. Just as non-western societies adopt western ideas in areas such as science, medicine, and engineering, it is "natural," so the argument goes, that they should adopt western ideas about human rights.

According to received wisdom, the West is the standard bearer of all things "advanced," and it would make sense for the "advanced" western perspective on human rights to be adopted by the rest of the world. This is seen as integral to national development and progress, as natural as the "right to life, liberty and security of person," as well as the prohibition of slavery.

Western countries now routinely tie the issue of human rights to their foreign policies, and particularly their relationships with non-western governments. The development agencies of western countries, such as the *United States International Development* (USID) agency, often use financial aid to non-western countries as "an instrument of diplomacy" to try to influence adherence to human rights "norms" as defined by western governments. Indeed, the dawn of the twenty-first century saw the emergence of a more "interventionist" policy by the United States, with the threat that non-western regimes that did not adhere to western human rights norms could be isolated, treated as "international pariahs," and even removed. "Regime change" became a recipe for dealing with non-western regimes deemed in violation of human rights. Thus, it would seem that human rights should become a powerful force for unity, at least among western powers and perhaps even globally among pro-democracy forces.

HUMAN RIGHTS AS A SOURCE OF CONFLICT

However, instead of becoming a force for global unity, the issue of human rights has become a force for disagreement and conflict. This is the first issue to resolve: why have human rights become so controversial on the international stage? We turn to this question in part one. In order to explain the controversies and criticisms revolving around human rights, I review three groups of critics.

First, some critics argue that the whole idea of "universal" human rights is misleading. They propose that rights and *duties*, what a person owes to others, are formulated and reformulated by majority groups, those who enjoy greater power. From this "relativist" perspective, rights and duties can and do vary across groups—there are no "universals" in this arena because whoever has greater power can determine what the "universals" are supposed to be and what rights and duties different groups of people have.

Second, various groups of traditionalists in different societies, including Islamic fundamentalists in both western and non-western societies, claim that what is claimed to be "universal human rights" actually contradicts their religions. This is particularly true with respect to the rights and duties of minorities, such as women, ethnic minorities, and gays. For example, for at least some Muslim fundamentalists, the issue of "equal treatment and freedom" for women and gays is explosive and something they are willing to sacrifice a great deal to fight against.

Third, many critics interpret the idea of "universal human rights" as a weapon that the western powers, particularly the United States, is using in order to intervene in the internal affairs of other countries. These critics argue that the United States is itself the greatest violator of human rights and selectively supports human rights when it is politically expedient to do so. Notoriously, the United States continues to support brutal dictatorships that are "pro-American," but to condemn other (sometimes more benign) regimes that are anti-American.

After reviewing the now heated international debate about human rights—a debate made ferocious by violence, barbarism, and terrorism on all sides—I argue that the principle of universal human rights is both correct and worth defending.

HUMAN RIGHTS FROM A RELATIVIST VIEW

Rights? Duties? Just in the last 10 years the world has witnessed two genocides in Rwanda and Bosnia; the war in the Congo characterized by the terrorization of civilians and the enlistment of child soldiers; traffic in slavery in southern Sudan; the mutilation of civilian populations by rebel armies in Sierra Leone; civilian deaths perpetrated by both sides in the Middle East; kidnapping, murders, and extortion by government forces in Cambodia and Chechnya; the use of torture in China and Turkey; the terrorist attacks on the World Trade Center in New York and the Pentagon in Washington, D.C.; and the death penalty in the United States and elsewhere . . . There is apparently no universally honored conception of human rights and duties.

This is how Winnifred Louis and Donald Taylor, two leading researchers based in Australia and Canada respectively, began their argument against the idea of universal human rights and in support of a relativist explanation.[5] Louis and Taylor offer a "strong relativist" perspective, arguing that by looking closely at differences across cultures at any one time, and at changes over time within a particular culture, the lack of universals in rights becomes clear. As we shall see, these are powerful arguments that have a lot of merit.

Consider how the rights of different groups have changed within western societies since the seventeenth century, and particularly after the great revolutionary movements in America and France at the end of the eighteenth century. Whereas before these changes, representative government and "the right to vote" were not reflected in national politics, after this revolutionary era these new rights were gradually expanded in most of Europe, even in England where the dominant policy was to introduce "a little change in a time of change." The parliamentary reforms of 1832 in England extended voting rights to many middle-class men, and the push toward greater rights in other western European countries resulted in new revolutions in most of western Europe in 1848. By the end of the nineteenth century, most white males had the right to vote in elections in the United States and Europe, and slavery has officially ended. Women and ethnic minorities won greater rights in the twentieth century, and from the 1960s a range of "equal rights" legislation strengthened the rights of most minority groups in western societies, including gays, people with physical disabilities, and native groups.

Clearly, what are considered as the "rights of men," "rights of women," and so on, changed a great deal across time in the same societies. For example, despite (often justified) criticisms about continued racism in the United States in the twenty-first century, the rights of an African-American in eighteenth century Alabama in United States, were drastically different from, and far inferior compared with the rights of an African-American in early twenty-first- century Alabama. There has been tremendous improvement in the area of rights for minorities, although there still exists some room for more improvement.

Rights across Cultures

Differences in rights are also clearly evident when we look across cultures at any one time.[6] For example, compare the rights of women and men in Islamic countries, such as Iran and Saudi Arabia, with Scandinavian countries, such as Sweden and Norway. Women in Scandinavian countries have equal rights, and government legislation is designed to maximize the possibility that women enjoy equality in practice as well as on paper. For example, when a woman gives birth to a baby, the father of the baby has generous paternity leave benefits (just as the mother has maternity leave benefits), so that father and mother have equal opportunities to take care of the infant(s), and there is more possibility to share the burdens and joys of childcare. Consequently, "family responsibilities" confront both mother and father in their pursuit of career goals (despite this, traditional gender roles continue to influence the behavior of Scandinavian women and men, but to a lesser degree than in most other countries).

Compare this with the situation in Iran and Saudi Arabia, where women lack many basic rights, both on paper and in practice, and according to formal law treated as second-class citizens. For whatever rights women have, men have more. This is symbolized by marriage rights: women can have one husband, but men can have four wives at any one time. Moreover, in addition to the four "permanent" wives allowed to all Muslim men, Shi'a Muslim men can have as many "temporary" wives as they like. A "temporary" marriage can last twenty minutes, twenty hours, twenty days, or even twenty years, there are no limitations in for how short or long time such marriage lasts. But, whereas men can have numerous wives at any one time, women can only have one husband at any one time.

Women are excluded from a number of important professions because they are not considered mentally and physically suitable. For example, women are not permitted to become judges because they are deemed as cognitively and emotionally unfit to judge cases. It is assumed that they become too emotionally involved and make incorrect, irrational decisions. Of course, this is not very different from the situation of women in medieval western societies, but it is very different from the equal rights enjoyed by women in twenty-first- century western societies.

Individualism and Rights

Just as differences in rights across cultures seem to strike a blow against the idea of universal rights, the modern preoccupation with individual rights seems to suggest that cultural factors are all important and universals are a myth in the domain of rights. After all, why just focus on individual rights? Why is there not a matched concern with collective rights? Critics contend that one reason why the *Universal Declaration of Human Rights* neglects collective rights is because this Declaration reflects Western and more specifically U.S. cultural concerns.

Research studies comparing levels of individualism across cultures around the world show that among the major societies, the United States is the most individualistic. This means that people in the United States are more likely to endorse the ethic of "self help," "individual responsibility," and "going it alone," as well as to have weaker links with groups, the family, and the community. The political scientist Robert Putnam has documented how Americans are increasingly "bowling alone" and becoming disconnected from community activities.[7] In practice, this means fewer people involved in neighborhood organizations, Girl Guides, Boy Scouts, and the likes.

Advanced technologies have accelerated this trend toward individu-alism and isolation from groups and communities. In the twenty-first century, young people in particular rely on varieties of electronic com-munications (e-mail, Instant Messenger, Face Book, Internet chat rooms, and so on) to communicate with others. These new communication sys-tems allow for electronic communities, involving individuals who might only infrequently meet face—to face, and might even remain anonymous (as in the case of chat room participants using adopted names). "Social-izing" in this new age can involve an individual sitting alone, "chatting" with strangers who she or he might never meet. Even when collective action is taken, through "eswarming" for example, individuals take ac-tion with unidentified others. Critics contend that this individualistic tendency among Americans is reflected in the neglect of collective rights and focus on individual rights in the *Universal Declaration of Human Rights*.

Neglect of Collective Duties

Also, the contemporary emphasis on "universal individual rights" goes hand in hand with a neglect of "universal collective duties,"[8] which concern the responsibilities of the group and the larger society to the individual, and perhaps the most important formal depiction of this is the responsibilities of governments to their citizens. Societies follow a range of strategies for how their governments deal with responsibilities toward citizens, from societies that believe in "small government" and little government intervention, to those that espouse a "from the cradle to the grave" support for citizens in education, health, and other key domains.

In the United States, there is a strong rhetoric of responsibilities being assigned to individual citizens rather than to the government. This has important consequences for American society. For example, the poor state of public transportation ("self-reliance" basically translates to most people having to have access to some form of private transportation), the lack of health care coverage for about 45 million people, and the enormous costs of higher education in America, all result from a tendency for successive U.S. administrations to limit government responsibilities and to give priority to the individual responsibilities of citizens—even when these citizens are children and are unable to earn money to cover health care and other costs. This "American tendency" toward neglecting collective duties to the individual seems to be reflected in the *Universal Declaration of Human Rights*, suggesting that human rights are local and cultural, rather than universal.

Related to these criticisms of the idea of "universal" human rights is the criticism that the modern concept of human rights is western and contradictory to certain major non-western value systems.

Human Rights as Contradicting Traditional Non-Western Values and as a Western Ploy

"The Justice Department has asked a federal appeals court to impose tighter restrictions on the hundreds of lawyers who represent detainees at Guantánamo Bay, Cuba . . . many of the lawyers say the restrictions would make it impossible to represent their clients . . . "

—William Glaberson[9] reporting in *The New York Times*

Public perception in most regions of the world, including in many parts of the United States, is that since the launch of the so-called "war on terror," the U.S. government has waged an endless war on basic human rights. Following an "ends justify the means" policy, which seems to mirror the behavior of terrorist groups, the U.S. government has turned its back on human rights. The treatment of prisoners at Guantánamo Bay is the most visible sign of this trend: at every turn, it seems, the U.S. government is determined to deny prisoners the rights that are assumed to be a basic and necessary part of "universal rights." This even includes denying prisoners access to lawyers, so that they can receive professional legal advice. But is what has been taking place since the terrorist attacks of 9/11 very different from past trends?

From Guantánamo Bay and Abu Ghraib prisons during the post-2003 invasion of Iraq, to the Mai Lai massacre and the use of agent orange and other inhuman weapons during the Vietnam war, to the internment of Japanese–Americans during World War II; from support for "pro-American" dictatorships (such as that of General Parvez Musharraf in Pakistan) in the twenty-first century, to support for dictatorships in Latin America and many other parts of the world for over half a century after World War II, there is no lack of distant and recent examples for critics to point out as support for the claim that the United States itself has failed to uphold human rights. Again and again, the U.S. government has shown it is willing to disregard human rights in order to fight those who it labels as "the enemy." This includes trampling on *Habeas Corpus* and other long-established "human rights" in the "war on terror."

Human Rights and U.S. Support for "Pro-American" Dictatorships

If Guantánamo Bay and Abu Ghraib prisons are the most visible "small scale" symbols of U.S. violation of human rights, American support for "pro-American" dictatorships is the clearest "large scale" symbol. Rather than being guided by human rights principles, U.S. policy seems to be guided by self-interest. For example, successive U.S. administrations, both Democrat and Republican, have supported dictatorships in Saudi Arabia, Kuwait, Egypt, and other countries of the Middle East region. This policy has been based on the assumption that support for dictatorships is the best way of ensuring access to cheaper and more reliable Middle East oil.

In other cases, the U.S. foreign policy has been guided by the idea of "the enemy of my enemy is my friend." For example, American support for the military dictatorship of General Musharraf in the twenty-first century is only the latest of a series of antidemocratic maneuvers. The United States stood firmly behind General Zia ul-Haq (1924–1988) when in 1977 he deposed the democratically elected government of Prime Minister Zulfiqar Ali Bhutto (1928–1979), hanged Bhutto, and maintained martial law until his own death in a mysterious plane crash in 1988. The U.S. support for dictatorships and acceptance of nuclear arms in Pakistan, have been designed as a counterbalance to India, a country that was seen as too left-leaning and too close to the Soviet Union. With the collapse of the Soviet Union, the U.S. policy has shifted to being slightly more supportive of India, as a counterbalance to the rapid growth of India's neighbor to the east, that is communist China.

Of course, the United States should be lauded for implementing the Marshall Plan, named after the Secretary of State George C. Marshall, which was initiated in 1947 and helped to preserve democracy in western Europe.[10] Democracy in Japan also is hugely indebted to the United States because it was through American support that Japan was rebuilt as a democracy after World War II (1939–1945). However, these examples do not negate the criticism that American support for democracy tends to be highly selective because democracy is supported when it serves American interests, but the U.S. government is just as likely to support a dictatorship and to ignore or even trample on human rights when American interests seem to require such behavior. Again and again, dictators have found that they can crush democratic opposition at home, with at least tacit U.S. support, if they can persuade American political leaders that this course of action is in the interests of the United States.

This "functional" policy of the United States toward human rights and democracy, whereby support is only given when it serves American interests, strengthens a relativist interpretation of human rights. This seems to be a classic case of human rights being whatever the most powerful forces say it is: might is right. Because the United States is the sole superpower in the first part of the twenty-first century, American governments can condemn "human rights abuses" in Iran, Syria, Cuba, Venezuela, and other countries deemed as "unfriendly" toward the United States, but ignore human rights abuses in Egypt, Saudi Arabia, and many other countries deemed as its "friends." If human rights can be manipulated by the powerful, if they can be used as a weapon against enemies and ignored to support "friends," the implication is that there is no such thing as universal human rights.

In addition to the argument that human rights are manipulated for political purposes to serve the interests of the powerful, some critics also argue that human rights, as currently understood and reflected in United Nations' documents and declarations, is a western product and contradicts foundational aspects of certain non-Western cultures and religions.

NATURAL LAW, POSITIVE LAW, AND "UNIVERSAL" HUMAN RIGHTS

Two contrasting traditions to understanding the sources and characteristics of law are represented by *natural law*, whereby rights and duties arise from divine sources and are discovered by humans, and *positive law*, whereby rights and duties are social constructions and reflect the cultural, political, and economic conditions of human societies. From both traditions, criticisms have been leveled against the idea of universal human rights. We have already discussed the relativist position arguing against universal human rights (it is appropriate to note that relativist critics are working within the framework of a positive law tradition). Next, we consider a number of criticisms that arise, sometimes directly, from a natural law tradition. On the surface, this seems contradictory, since the natural law tradition would appear to be completely aligned with the idea of universal rights and duties. After all, divine law would seem naturally to cover all humans, and thus the issue of relativism would seem to be overcome. Indeed, there might be no problem at all if there existed only one natural law tradition but, as is argued below, there are multiple such traditions.

"Western" Human Rights Contradict Major Non-Western Religions and Cultures

The natural law tradition seems, on the surface at least, to side step a major stumbling block created by the positive law tradition. Researchers following the positive law tradition have for the most part come to positions supporting varying degrees of relativism. If human rights and duties are socially constructed, then we should expect variations across cultures, depending on political, economic, and other characteristics of societies. From this perspective, it seems there is little hope of agreement on universal human rights and duties. Even if such agreement is reached, it is based on social conventions that have no universal, context-independent validity and can routinely and perhaps legitimately be broken by reference to local interests and normative systems.

In contrast, the positive law tradition seems to provide a solid basis for universal rights and duties. If the ultimate source of law is divine, then, as part of the natural order of the world, the same rights and duties apply to all humans. Moreover, divine laws do not change over time, but apply to all humans in all eras. However, on closer inspection, it becomes clear that natural law does not solve the problem of relativism.

Indeed, paradoxically perhaps, the natural law position on rights and duties actually magnifies the problem of relativism. This is because just as there are a variety of different religions, there are also multiple different "natural laws." In essence, it is more accurate to use the term "natural laws" in the plural than to refer it in the singular sense. Thus, there are different groups of religious people who actively support different "natural laws" that in some important respects contradict one another.

Moreover, the "natural laws" arising from each of the different religious traditions have adherents who devoutly believe that their religion, and only their religion, represents the one and only valid faith, and that their natural law, and only their natural law, is the one and only valid natural law. Indeed, religious fanatics from each of the different traditions tend to dogmatically reject the claims of other religious traditions and to sometimes be willing to kill followers of other religions, and to die to defend or further extend the influence of their own religious tradition. The rise in Islamic terrorism is just one indication of this tendency.

It could be argued that the followers of the major religious traditions have a number of core values in common, such as their opposition to abortion, feminism, and gay rights. These "common beliefs" or "core values" could be used to establish a set of universal rights and duties. There is some validity to this claim, particularly when the claim is considered purely on its logical merit. However, the psychological merit of this claim is weak, because ultimately the supporters of the different religious traditions are more strongly motivated, sometimes consciously, to differentiate their own group from others and to demonstrate the superiority of their group in comparison with others than to establish similarities between their group and other religions.

Besides, the core values of the major religions, rather than remaining fixed and timeless, tend to change over time. Consider, for example, how the core values of Christianity have shifted over the last 2,000 years or so, with the Reformation influenced by Martin Luther (1483–1546) representing just one major shift. Luther's attack on the papal system, his marriage to Katherine von Bora, an ex-nun who had abandoned the conventional life of a nun, his ninety-five theses attacking the papal practice of indulgences (which were famously nailed up on the church door at Wittenberg), all symbolized and sparked a shift in the relationship between the people and the Christian Church. Dramatic changes also have come about in our era. Since the final decades of the twentieth century, at least some Christian groups are more tolerant toward certain minorities, such as women and gays. There are even Christian churches where women and openly gay men are permitted to become priests. These changes in Christianity suggest that natural law also changes, across time and place.

Positive Law: A Cultural Evolutionary Perspective on Human Rights

We have seen that the idea of universal human rights is being attacked from different directions. The attacks have come from left-leaning critics who argue that those who enjoy greater power can define and manipulate human rights to suit their particular interests, and that human rights are being used as a weapon against those who have less power. The attacks have also emanated from right-wing defenders of traditional cultures in both western and non-western societies, who argue that human rights are a modern liberal creation that tries to overturn conservative value systems by giving legitimacy to a gay lifestyle for example. Does this mean that there is no basis on which we can claim there to be universal rights and duties?

I believe that the research evidence clearly demonstrates universal roots to human rights and duties. My approach to addressing this issue is not based on natural law, or on the narrow kind of sociobiology or evolutionary psychology[11] that has captured the imagination of a sizable number of researchers and also the lay public. Rather, my approach combines cultural and biological processes in evolution. I begin by pointing out that in order for our ancestors to succeed on our own long evolutionary path, they had to develop a number of *primitive social relations*, elementary behaviors that evolved as part of a repertoire of skills necessary for group survival. Earlier (in Chapters 3 and 4) I discussed turn-taking, empathy, and trust as examples of universal primitive social relations. It is useful to consider the evolutionary roots of such behaviors.

If primitive social relations are a product of evolutionary processes, we should be able to find traces of them in animal behavior. Indeed, there is evidence that we can. There is mounting evidence that through games and early activities, animals are socialized to learn a sense of fairness.[12] Animals react negatively to unfairness; for example, play breaks down when an animal in a group does not follow the rules of a game. In a fascinating study on monkeys reacting to "unequal pay," researchers showed that monkeys who received a lower reward (a grape instead of a preferred cucumber) for the same "work" reacted by becoming uncooperative. Some animals also seem to be able to empathize with others who they have bonded with. Researchers found that mice behaved in ways that could be interpreted as showing empathy when they witnessed their cagemates experience pain, but they did not show the same reaction when mice that were strangers to them experienced the same pain.[13]

One interpretation of this line of research is that through evolution, animals and humans have evolved to have an inbuilt "moral grammar."[14] There is no doubt that our biological makeup enable us to become moral animals, but biology and brain are simply enablers. What brings our human moral system to fruition is our collective life and culture.

CONCLUDING COMMENT

The concept of universal human rights should ideally serve as a unifier, bringing all humankind together under a banner of fairness and justice. In practice, however, human rights have proven to be a divider, and in the case of Islamic communities human rights are serving as a serious threat.

One reason for this situation is the perceived hypocrisy of U.S. foreign policy. Human rights are now seen by many people around the world as a weapon that the United States in particular is using to attack others when it suits American purposes. People in the United States might have forgotten about prisoners held without trial at Guantánamo Bay and torture at Abu Ghraib and its other facilities (some outside U.S. borders), but much of the rest of the world has not forgotten.[15]

Human rights are also seen as a weapon used by the United States to place pressure on regimes that demonstrate independence and wish to go their own way. Thus, the United States attacks dictatorships in Iran, Syria, and Cuba for "human rights abuses," but supports many other dictatorships that abuse human rights because although they are "dictatorships that trample on human rights" they are "our dictatorships."

PART THREE

The New Global
American Dilemma

In the preceding chapters, the main argument I have presented is that terrorism can be best understood from a cultural evolutionary perspective, with the following four points being central to this perspective.

1. In the course of evolution, involving animals, plants, as well as humans, there develop competition between life forms seeking scarce resources that enhance their chances of survival.
2. In conditions where competing life forms experience sudden contact and where one or both groups have low preadaptiveness, catastrophic evolution can result. Consequently, one or both groups can experience decline and even extinction.
3. Groups experiencing sudden contact react through a wide variety of defensive strategies to enhance their survival chances. The defense mechanisms adopted can vary considerably in characteristics (e.g., how aggressive or peaceful a tactic is) and also in outcomes (i.e., with respect to how effective and adaptive a tactic actually proves to be).
4. Among the many defensive strategies adopted by human groups perceiving serious external threat are radicalization and terrorism.

On the basis of the perspective outlined above, terrorism can be interpreted as an extreme evolutionary-developed reaction to out-group threat, and the perceived possibility of in-group annihilation. Of course, it would be a gross misinterpretation to view this analysis as in any way a support for or endorsement of terrorism.[1] This would be like endorsing rape as a strategy for passing on one's genes.

The process of evolution is itself morally neutral. The "winners" in evolutionary terms are simply the life forms that reproduce faster. Those who survive are not morally any better (or worse) than those who become extinct. But, we humans can and do make moral judgments about alternative evolutionary paths, identifying some paths as better than others. Thus, at the same time as interpreting terrorism as a defense mechanism adopted by groups fearful of their own extinction, it is correct and justified that we condemn terrorism in all its various shapes and forms.

The condemnation of terrorism is consistent with the upholding of human rights more broadly, based on the idea that there are certain basic rights and duties shared by all humans.[2]

In this final section of the book, my focus is on the global context and the role of the United States in the larger world. This role has often been shaped by the need for short-term "quick fixes" that would be achieved before the next political elections come around. Of course, short-term solutions to terrorism must be adopted, as I have argued earlier in this book and elsewhere,[3] because we must respond to actual terrorist attacks as well as threats of attacks. However, even more important are long-term, foundational solutions that get at the deeper roots of terrorism and radicalization. Such long-term solutions involve changing aspects of the global situation, and particularly the role of the United States in the global context.

Global solutions to terrorism inevitably involve the United States, and require changes in U.S. policy at the global level. In Chapter 9, I explore how the role of the United States has subtly shifted, and there is now a *new global American dilemma*. This new global American dilemma is not dependent on local politics; irrespective of whether a Republican or Democrat occupies the White House; the United States has shifted into a new role, one that will be taken up in the longer term, just as the American dilemma of race had to be confronted domestically.

The confrontation of the new global American dilemma will lead to "women as the long-term solution" to Islamic terrorism, and this is examined in the "Afterward" section. I argue that gradual but definite increased participation of Muslim women in higher education and in labor force could result in a far stronger Islamic women's movement, one that demands greater rights for Muslim women. If this path is taken, the outcome of changes in the role of women outside the home could be a transformation in Muslim families, and the larger Muslim society. At the same time, however, we should keep in mind that participation of women in higher education does not necessarily result in the empowerment of women in the public sphere and in the labor market.

CHAPTER 9

The American Dilemma
Becomes Global

"We hold these truths to be self-evident: That all men are created equal; that they are endowed by their creator with certain inalienable rights; that among these are life, liberty, and the pursuit of happiness..."

These inspiring and immortal words, an essential part of the *Declaration of American Independence* (1776), are penned by Thomas Jefferson (1743–1826), one of the founding fathers of the American nation. Unfortunately Jefferson never acted decisively to resolve what should have been an obvious contradiction: he owned several hundred slaves and did not see fit to free them all, even as a last gesture in his final will (he did free two in his lifetime and five in his will). Clearly, in practice "all men are not created equal" in Jefferson's world, but this did not prevent Jefferson from preaching equality with sublime passion and eloquence.

When one visits "Monticello," the home that Jefferson designed and had built for himself in his native Virginia, the brilliance and elegance of Jefferson's mind come through, but the overwhelming spirit haunting the home is that of the hundreds of slaves who were owned by Jefferson and lived and worked on the grounds of his home and the surrounding countryside—always in captivity. One leaves Monticello with an uncomfortable feeling that the place represents contradictions, between lofty ideals and earthly practices. No amount of grand declarations can wipe away the cruelty and injustice of slavery, and the barbaric system that treated one group of humans like chattel but created luxurious personal benefits for Jefferson and others like him.

The rift between the American Creed and the American way of life, between expressed ideals and actual practices, has continued to haunt American society. This rift was famously examined by the Swedish economist Gunnar Myrdal (1898–1987), in a landmark study published under the title of *An American Dilemma* (1944).[4] Writing well before the era of desegregation and the revolutionary changes that followed in the United States during the 1960s, Myrdal argued that White Americans experienced a dilemma because of a monstrous contradiction between their actual mistreatment of African-Americans, even after the official end of slavery, and the "American Creed" espoused by mainstream America. The American Creed involves,

> ... ideals of the essential dignity of the individual human being, of the fundamental equality of all men, and of certain inalienable rights to freedom, justice, and a fair opportunity.... [5]

These glorious ideas are explicitly and proudly manifested in documents such as the *Declaration of American Independence*, the *United States Constitution*, and pioneering publications such as *The Federalist Papers* (originally published 1787–1788).[6] A problem is that even after the official end of slavery in the United States, African-Americans lived segregated lives, as second-class citizens and with very limited opportunities for upward social mobility.

The seminal contribution of Myrdal to this debate is that he pinpointed the contradiction or "dilemma" in the American position. The same nation cannot on the one hand espouse equality, freedom, and a value system based on *meritocracy*, where the position of individuals is determined by their personal contributions (rather than family ties and group memberships), but on the other hand practices race-based segregation and exclusion. A kind of collective cognitive dissonance will inevitably arise from this situation: the contradiction between beliefs and actions will result in increasingly intense anxiety and distress.

Whereas the original theory of cognitive dissonance put forward by Leon Festinger[7] (1919–1989) had focused on the processes within individual human minds, there are reasons to believe that Festinger's analysis is too narrow. For example, behavior that seems to suggest dissonance has since been reported in animals,[8] the implication being that in some situations what seems from the outside to be dissonance does not involve complex higher-order cognitive processes (unless we are willing to ascribe complex higher-order cognitive processes to animals). Second, it is reasonable to assume that some forms of dissonance as described by Festinger can be experienced by a society collectively as well as an individual. The collective experience of dissonance is certainly suggested by Myrdal's analysis.

COLLECTIVE COGNITIVE DISSONANCE IN THE UNITED STATES

Myrdal's analysis predicted the collective dissonance that people in the United States would experience. Myrdal believed this collective dissonance would arise as a result of incongruity between, first, the American meritocratic value system that espouses all people to be free and enjoy equality of opportunity and, second, the widespread practice of racial segregation that was practiced in the United States at least until the 1960s. But is it inevitable that such "dilemma" would result in a high enough level of dissonance that it would have to be resolved, either by changing the American practices that support group-based inequalities, or changing the American value system that supports freedom and equality of opportunities? Put more simply, would the contradiction between what Americans say and what they do on the issue of race become so distressing that it would lead Americans to change either what they do or what they say, or perhaps both? One answer is "yes," it is inevitable, and the evidence is that the dissonance experienced by American society led to the turbulence of the 1960s, desegregation, and equal opportunities legislation. At least on paper, African-Americans and other minorities now enjoy equal rights.

But one can also find evidence for a very different story line interpreting this situation. First, some would point to inequalities in important domains such as education[9] and argue that racism continues in the twenty-first century, but now through subtler symbolic forms. From this perspective, the "American dilemma" has only been resolved on paper, because although according to formal law everyone is equal, in practice inequalities persist. Second, on a more foundational level, one might challenge the idea that societies find it difficult to live with contradictory practices and values.

Living With Societal Contradictions

In practice, we can find many examples of societies living with inconsistent practices and values. For example, consider the idea of equality of opportunities, not in relation to race but in relations to social class (which is far broader than race). The rhetoric of "equality of opportunity" in the United States suggests that education should serve as a ladder, with all individuals having educational opportunities based on their personal characteristics, not their family wealth and connections. An "open access" educational system is supposed to be the motor behind the "American Dream." In practice, however, the American educational system is strongly biased in favor of the privileged, the fact being routinely reported in the mass media.[10] For example, I pick up today's *New York Times* and read the following in a report entitled "Ivy-League Letdown,"[11]

"In 2004, Lawrence Summers, then Harvard's president, pointed out that three-fourths of the students at selective colleges come from the top income quartile and only 9 percent from the bottom two quartiles combined."

This article continues in the following manner:

"In a society that claims to believe in equal opportunity, our top universities should lead by example. The scandalous fact is that between 2004 and 2006—an era of enormous wealth accumulation—27 of the 30 top-ranked college[s] saw a decline in the percentage of low-income (Pell-grant-eligible) students."

The outcome of this situation is that, "Low-income students earn bachelor's degrees at less than one-third the rate of high[-]income students." Given this "inequality of opportunity," and the enormous and increasing disparity between the richest and the poorest groups in the United States, why has dissonance not arisen to a level high enough to result in a change in either action or rhetoric, or both? Why is it that American politicians can still get away with claims that the United States is the land of "equal opportunities," when rich and poor clearly have unequal opportunities in America?[12] The answer is that this situation can continue as long as there is an effective "story" that most people buy into to justify the present inequalities.[13]

Cognitively Justifying the Existing Sociopolitical System

What kind of "story" is serving this dissonance-avoiding function in the United States? According to an intriguing modern theory,[14] the stories that dominate American culture lead to a justification of the present sociopolitical system, even at the expense of the self and the in-group. Despite group-based inequalities that work against most individuals, the world is interpreted as fair through a system of cognitive compensation. Stereotypes play an important role here. For example, people see it as more congruent to believe the poor to be happy ("Those people do not make much money, but they have a warm and loving family life") and the rich to be unhappy ("What good is all that money to them when they have such troubled family lives?"). Similarly, the highly talented are often depicted in a way that balances out their advantages over the less talented, "Most beautiful rich film actresses are miserable at heart; they have such terrible private lives."

Clearly, then, cognitive dissonance can be avoided even in situations where actions and beliefs are inconsistent, as long as there is a persuasive story that interprets the world as fair. So, we have to be careful not to assume that contradictory actions and values will always result in a person or a group feeling they have to change either their actions or values, or both. The system of slavery was interpreted as "fair" by generations of Americans, until the contradiction between slavery and espoused American values reached a climax in the American Civil War.

Will the same kind of dissonance arise at the global level?

AMERICAN IDEALS AND PRACTICES ON THE WORLD STAGE

"Though W. [sic] H[h]as made the issue of the progress of women in the Middle East a central part of 'the freedom agenda'... he doesn't seems bothered that 17 years after his father protected the Saudis when Saddam invaded Kuwait, Saudi women still can't drive or publicly display hair or skin and still get beheaded and lashed because of archaic laws. Neither does the female secretary of state of the United States."

—Dowd[15]

This is how the author Maureen Dowd highlighted a contradiction between what "W," President George W. Bush, has said about freedom in the Middle East, and what the actual situation continues to be like in the Middle East. Dowd's commentary came as part of the reporting on President Bush's tour of the Middle East in January 2008. Of course, President George W. Bush's tour of the Middle East received more critical attention because he led the United States to invade Iraq in 2003 and failed to implement effective policies during the occupation phase of the war. However, rather than focus on the failings of this particular president, my concern is with a more general issue to do with all post–World War II U.S. policy in the Middle East, irrespective of whether a Democrat or Republican was in the White House.

A key reason why President George W. Bush has been castigated very severely by critics is because he has (inadvertently) put the spotlight on the contradiction between ideals and practices in American foreign policy (of course, many American voters never forgave Bush for "winning" the 2000 presidency with only 47 percent of the popular vote compared to

Vice President Al Gore, who gained 48 percent. The intervention of the U.S. Supreme Court meant that Bush eventually received a higher number of electoral votes, even though Gore received a higher percentage of the popular vote). Bush has been stridently raising the issue of democracy and freedom, and espousing support for democracy in all countries, including in the Middle East. This strategy has put the spotlight on the contradiction between American policies of supporting dictatorships around the world, but only when the dictators in question are thought to serve American interests. The principle of American foreign policy has continued to be, "dictators and torturers are good guys when they are our dictators and torturers, otherwise they are part of the axis of evil."

In this way, irrespective of whether it is a Democrat or Republican in the White House, the United States has supported dictatorships in Asia, Africa, and Latin America. During the Cold War years of rivalry with the Soviet Union, the "reasoning" behind U.S. support for dozens of bloody dictatorships was that "the ends" of defeating communism justified the "means" (of supporting dictatorships that crushed left-wing movements). It could be argued that history proved this strategy to be correct because the Soviet Union and communism were ultimately defeated, the "Iron Curtain" crashed to the ground, and Eastern Europe gained freedom and democracy. Also, in the crucial energy-rich regions of the Near and Middle East, American-supported dictatorships prevented the Soviet empire from reaching the Persian Gulf and gaining control of the strategically vital Strait of Hormuz, through which tankers transport oil to fuel western economies.

From this perspective, the Soviet invasion of Afghanistan in 1979 demonstrated that the communist threat was real, and that every means possible had to be employed to defeat communism. Support for dictatorships in Saudi Arabia, Iran, and other key states of the region was a necessary price to pay for defending western interests against communism.

"The Ends Justify the Means" U.S. Foreign Policy

According to this "the ends justify the means" thinking, it is also legitimate to use Islam as a tool to fight communism. Indeed, one of the most effective weapons against "atheist" communists is religious fundamentalist, and in the Near and Middle East the fundamentalists, to be used against communism, are, of course, Muslims, because the vast majority of the population in the region are Muslims. Thus, after the Soviet invasion of Afghanistan, the United States helped to strengthen Muslim-fundamentalist movements in the Near East and Middle East region, and this included support for Islamic fundamentalists who gathered to repel Soviet forces from Afghanistan.

Again, in defense of "the ends justify the means" policy of the United States to support Islamic fundamentalism in the Near and Middle East particularly in the late 1970s and 1980s, it could be claimed that the policy worked: the Soviets were defeated in Afghanistan. However, the Islamic fundamentalists who defeated the communists also eventually establish the Taliban government in Afghanistan—and the crimes of the Taliban regime against humanity are clear to all thinking people. Both inside and outside Afghanistan, the Taliban regime directly and indirectly committed vile crimes. Of course, defenders of American foreign policy would still claim that the coming to power of the Taliban was a small price to pay for achieving victory over the Soviets; a small regional defeat (the coming to power of the Taliban) had to be tolerated in order to achieve a much larger global victory (collapse of the Soviet empire).

A "goals justify the means" policy is also extended to explain continued U.S. support for dictatorships in the Near and Middle East in the twenty-first century. After all, there is increased competition between countries, including the newly emerging "giants of Asia," China and India, for oil, gas, and other resources concentrated in the Near and Middle East. Approximately one billion "new consumers" (people who can afford to purchase cars, washing machines, dish washers, televisions, and other goods that have become part of the middle-class American lifestyle) are about to be added to the numbers of existing consumers on the global market. Most of these "new consumers" are from China, India, Brazil, and other "developing nations." This huge surge in consumer demand will dramatically increase competition for energy resources over the next two decades.[16] The U.S. policy of keeping in power Near and Middle East dictators who are "our dictators" will ensure American domination of energy resources, squeezing out the Indians and Chinese in particular.

This same logic is applied to justify the U.S.-led invasion of Iraq, a country with oil reserves that rival those of Saudi Arabia. The United States can use Iraq as a platform to launch military operations in the rest of the region, to defend its interests whenever they are threatened. The short-term failure of the occupation and the mess created by the insurgency, the scandal of Abu Ghraib, and the like are not important, because through the invasion of Iraq the United States has taken military control of not only Iraq's energy resources, but also the region generally. According to this logic, the loss of hundreds of thousands of Iraqi lives and thousands of American lives is tragic, but it is just a collateral damage that cannot be avoided in such circumstances.

DEMOCRATS, REPUBLICANS, AND THE NEW GLOBAL AMERICAN DILEMMA

The controversial two-term (2000–2008) presidency of George W. Bush has created the impression that American foreign policy has dramatically changed since 2000. The counterproductive reaction of the Bush administration to the tragedy of 9/11, the launching of the seemingly endless "war on terror," the terrible conflict-based relationship between the United States and Iran, as well as a range of other "hallmark" features of the Bush policy, seem to mark the post-2000 period as unique. A widely held assumption is that if a Democrat had been in the White House, American foreign policy would have developed in a very different direction, even if 9/11 and all other events had remained the same. But the fact is that in one key aspect, irrespective of whether a Democrat or a Republican was in the White House, U.S. policy toward developing-world dictatorships has remained the same since World War II (1939–1945).

There has been very little difference between Democratic and Republican American presidents in their continued support for dictatorships in the developing world, and this is especially true in the Near and Middle East. Consider, for example, the consistently supportive U.S. policies toward dictatorship in Saudi Arabia under Democratic and Republican presidents. Indeed, the sharpest change in "policy" has come in the form of new "pro-democracy" rhetoric used by president George W. Bush, who has specifically urged for democratic changes in Saudi Arabia, although he has not in practice changed U.S. policies so as to bring about democratic changes in that country. However, by changing the rhetoric of U.S. foreign policy, President George W. Bush cast the spotlight on the new global American dilemma. By talking about democracy in Saudi Arabia, President Bush brought into sharp focus American policies in support of the Saudi dictators.

Rhetorical Focus on Freedom

Even in his final State of the Union Address, President Bush kept the spotlight on freedom and democracy, stating that "We trust that people, when given the chance, will choose a future of freedom. . . . "[17] The problem is that people in the rest of the world view American support for dictatorships in Saudi Arabia, Egypt, Kuwait, and other "pro-American" countries as the greatest obstacle to freedom and democracy. This perception of America as an obstacle to freedom and democracy has strengthened with every speech that President Bush and his associates have made in support of freedom and democracy, while at the same time continuing the policy of supporting dictatorships.

It could be argued that James (Jimmy) Carter, president of the United States from 1976–1980 was a Democrat who supported democracy in the Near and Middle East. President Carter did make many speeches about human rights. However, it would be naive to assume that Carter's rhetoric actually improved human rights in the Near and Middle East. True, Carter's policies were in large part responsible for the rapidity of the collapse of the Shah's dictatorial regime in Iran because the perception in Iran was that Carter was pulling the rug out from underneath the Shah by telling the Iranian military to step aside and drop their support for the Shah. The sudden disappearance of the central power in Iran left a vacuum that was filled by the only group organized enough to take over, and that was Khomeini's Islamic fundamentalist movement, which used the mosques as local headquarters for its foot soldiers.

The rapid change in Iran from a monarchic dictatorship to a theocratic dictatorship provides an important lesson for the United States, as American policy makers try to meet the challenge of the new global American dilemma. Secular democratic opposition to dictatorship must be allowed to grow, and even nourished, by the United States. This is the only means of avoiding the transition directly from one form of dictatorship to another, the "Turban for the Crown" as happened in Iran.

When secular democratic opposition is not permitted to grow, as is the case in Saudi Arabia, Egypt, Kuwait, and most of the Near and Middle East, the only political movement that will thrive in this vacuum is Islamic fundamentalism. This is because the dictators of the Near and Middle East can close down all other institutions, including schools and universities, but they cannot close down mosques. A consequence is that mosques become a haven for political activists, and all permitted political opposition takes shape in the framework provided by Islamic extremists. This is exactly what happened in Iran, and there is a serious danger of this taking place in Egypt and some other Near and Middle Eastern societies. The Muslim Brotherhood is gaining power in Egypt and a number of other societies in the region, because young people who want to be politically active only have this one channel to work through, all other paths are closed to them.

Thus, the new global American dilemma is coming into sharp focus, as Islamic fundamentalism increasingly gains strength and becomes the motor for collective action particularly among the young in "pro-American" Near and Middle Eastern dictatorships propped up by Washington, DC. What can the United States do in response to this new challenge? In addressing this question, we are forced to delve deeper into the irrational nature of much of human behavior, including U.S. foreign policy.

Irrationalism and U.S. Foreign Policy

By far the greatest advantage that the United States enjoys over its competitors for world dominance in the twenty-first century is "soft power": the strong magnetic pull of American culture, particularly the appeal of popular American culture among young people around the world. In just about every society, the young are strongly influenced by and attracted toward American culture, including music, films, novels, and clothes coming from the United States. This is the case even in societies with outspoken anti-American governments, such as the Islamic Republic of Iran and Venezuela under the leadership of President Hugo Chavez.

Scratch beneath the surface of the fundamentalist regime in Tehran, and one quickly gets to tens of millions of Iranian youth who are eager to get a visa to visit America or even move to live in America. This includes members of the newly affluent ruling class in Iran, who continue to use religion to keep tight control over the reigns of power. Many of these new "thousand ruling families" have accumulated substantial properties and bank accounts in western countries and have relatives in the United States. Thus, the "death to America" rhetoric of the mobs the regime puts out on Tehran streets stands in sharp contrast with the magnetic pull that American culture continues to exert on many of the younger generation in Iran.

A similar situation exists in Venezuela, where Chavez and his supporters keep up a stream of anti-American rhetoric. I was lecturing at Caracas University in 2002, at a time when Hugo Chavez was on the ascent, concentrating power and mobilizing the "barefoot masses" behind him by focusing on the "military threat from the United States" (much as Ayatollah Khomeini and other hardliners in Iran have mobilized the "barefoot masses" by focusing attention on the military threat of the "Great Satan," America). At the time when Chavez supporters poured into the streets daily and filled the air with anti-American slogans, the "soft power" of America was clearly overwhelming in the everyday activities of the people. The magic of Hollywood cannot be denied, even by Hugo Chavez and Ayatollah Khomeini.

But, in order for the United States to take advantage of its soft-power domination around the world, American foreign policy must be designed to maximize contact with societies such as Cuba, Venezuela, and

Iran. Unfortunately, such a "cold, calculated" approach has been overwhelmed by the irrational, emotion-based reactions of American policy makers. This can be illustrated by considering the case of Iran–American relations.

IRAN AND AMERICA ON THE COUCH

Iran and America are patients sorely in need of therapy. Both have been traumatized by a number of tragic events during their dysfunctional relationship, including the hostage-taking crisis of 1979 and the terrorist attacks of 9/11 (of course, Iran was not responsible for the 9/11 terrorist attacks against the United States, but this tragic event served to bolster anti-Iranian sentiments in America as part of the irrational displacement of aggression process that took place through the leadership of President George W. Bush). The couch is waiting, and the patients, Iran and America, need to cooperate.

But there is strong resistance to cooperation and vested interests on both sides prefer to continue the experience of trauma, mutual distrust, fear, and out-group aggression. Authoritarian factions in both the United States and in Iran immediately launch frenzied attacks against any of their members who dare to make "unauthorized" contact with the other side, particularly contact that might imply normalization of relations.[18] This trend is illustrated by the following incident, which reflects the high level of distrust and even paranoia among the authoritarian factions of both groups, "White House officials expressed anger on Tuesday about an appearance in which the U.S. ambassador to the United Nations . . . sat beside the Iranian foreign minister at a panel of the World Economic Forum in Davos, Switzerland. . . . "[19]

On the Iranian side, also, any Iranian seen to be in contact with American officials outside the strict framework provided by authoritarian factions is immediately lambasted. These authoritarian factions are motivated by strong vested interests to conjure up "incidents" that ensure greater military friction between Iran and the United States, because it is only in a condition of permanent conflict (such as that created by the endless "war on terror") that authoritarians can gain and maintain power.

Another "Incident"

On Sunday January 6, 2008, three U.S. warships were in international waters in the strategically vital Strait of Hormuz, through which Middle East oil tankers have to pass to supply fuel to the world, when they were suddenly approached by five Iranian speedboats. What happened next is in dispute, with the United States and the Islamic Republic of Iran propagating different and competing accounts of events, and even providing the world with their own videos of the incident to back their version of what happened.[20] According to American accounts, as the Iranian speedboats approached, the Iranians sent a message via the internationally known bridge-to-bridge radio channel, warning that, " . . . you will explode in a few minutes."[21] American officials, led by President George W. Bush, were quick to condemn the Iranian actions, using labels such as "reckless" and "provocative," Apparently, the American ships were about to fire on the speedboats when the Iranians suddenly steered away and avoided a clash.

Iranian officials, on the other hand, played down the incident and said it was not significant. Indeed, an Iranian Foreign Ministry spokesman described the event as "an ordinary incident, which happens now and then for both sides". Iran described the American video of the event as "fabricated" and claimed that no threats had been made from Iranian naval vessels.

The U.S. Navy is particularly concerned that Iran might attempt to "swarm" much larger, more powerful American ships using multiple speedboats. In 2000, a small boat attack against the U.S. destroyer Cole, docked at the time for refueling in Yemen, caused considerable damage and the death of seventeen American sailors. But that was a terrorist attack and not a confrontation between the navies of two sovereign states.

Another reminder of the threat posed by Iran's "swarming" naval tactic came in a war game carried out by the U.S. military in August 2002. During that war game, titled the "Millennium Challenge 2002" and carried out in the Persian Gulf, the United States lost sixteen warships, including an aircraft carrier. The enemy relied on the sheer numbers of speedboats to overwhelm American defenses.

An Eternal Dynamic: External Threat Leads to Internal Cohesion

There is not doubt, then, about the seriousness of the threat facing the United States in the Gulf region. But since the 1978 revolution in Iran, the confrontations between the United States and Iran have involved words and not deeds, verbal missiles and not actual ones. The two sides have put their energies into the task of gaining a better position and "looking better" on the world stage.[22]

The important question to ask is, what purpose do such confrontations serve? In March 2007, Iran's Revolutionary Guards captured fifteen British sailors in, what the British claim was, international waters in the Gulf and tensions between Iran and the West were raised once again. The British sailors were released unharmed after two weeks, but why were they captured in the first place? To answer this question, we need to examine closely the role that external threats play in in-group and intergroup dynamics in the new global village.

First, both historical cases and experimental evidence suggest that external threat leads to the rise of leaders who are perceived to be "strong," "resolute," and who aggressively defend in-group interests.[23] For example, it was in large part the Nazi threat that resulted in Winston Churchill (1874–1965) becoming Prime Minister in Britain, just as the Falklands war and the threat posed by the Irish Republican Army (IRA) helped Margaret Thatcher keep her position as prime minister for eleven and a half years. Churchill and Thatcher were both viewed by a majority of the British electorate as being strong leaders who can effectively guide the nation in times of grave danger.

Second, by highlighting threats from external enemies, fundamentalists, both in Iran and the in the United States, have found that they can gain greater public support for authoritarian and aggressive policies. This is a general trend in human behavior, clearly evident in modern societies experiencing terrorist threats. For example, researchers[24] found increased support for authoritarian policies among the Spanish public after the deadly March 11, 2004, terrorist attacks on passenger trains in Madrid. As a general strategy, politicians highlight "threats" to increase support for their policies. An analysis of the eight State Union Addresses delivered in 2001–2008 by President George W. Bush shows that he cited terror/terrorists and Iraq, two external threats, and taxes, an "internal threat" (from a conservative perspective), more often than other key words or phrases including health care, medicare, energy, social security, economy, jobs, and deficits.[25] Mr. Bush enjoyed by far the highest approval rating of his presidency during two periods when the American public was utterly focused on external threats: the 9/11 terrorist attacks and the 2003 U.S.-led war in Iraq.

A third important role of external threat is to shut down internal dissent and diminish civil liberties. There are three aspects to this trend. First, as a result of external threat there is increased pressure for everyone to conform within the in-group. Those who seem to be different become a target of suspicion and aggression. The blacklisting of suspected communist sympathizers in the United States in the 1950s and the internment of Japanese-Americans during World War II are well-known examples. But a more recent example is the silent conformity of mass media in the United States, in the face of false assertions by President George W. Bush and his administration, that Iraq had an active program to develop weapons of mass destruction (WMDs). During the buildup and immediately after the 2003 U.S.-led invasion of Iraq, even *The New York Times* and other major media outlets conformed to the false storyline that Saddam Hussein had stockpiled WMDs. Second, as a result of external threat there is greater support for antidemocratic government policies. For example, the public becomes more willing to abdicate civil liberties.[26] Third, external threat results in greater discrimination against minorities. For example, since the terrorist attacks of 9/11, prejudice against Arabs became stronger than prejudice against African Americans in the United States.[27]

In summary, then, by highlighting external threats, authoritarian factions within a group (for example within Iran and the United States) can

– increase public support for strong, aggressive leadership,
– silence dissenting voices and weaken liberal positions,
– increase pressure on and isolate minorities,
– diminish public opposition to the curtailing of civil liberties.

CONCLUDING COMMENT

Basic contradictions between United States rhetoric about "supporting democracy around the world" and U.S. actions in support of "friendly" dictatorships has created a new global American dilemma. By making the rhetoric of "spreading democracy" a centerpiece of his administration's policies, President George W. Bush inadvertently drew greater attention to contradictions between U.S. rhetoric and policies. President George W. Bush's plummeting popularity was in part a result of him acting as a mirror, allowing Americans to see their own image more clearly—and most Americans do not like the contradictions they see in American foreign policy, just as at one time most Americans were unhappy with the contradictions they saw between the practice of slavery and the rhetoric of equality found in the *Declaration of American Independence* and other foundational American documents.

The first American dilemma, arising out of the contradiction between the domestic practice of racial segregation and the rhetoric of equality, resulted in Americans rethinking their identity and asking, "What is an American? What kind of society is America?" The new global American dilemma is raising the same questions again and forcing Americans to deal with uncomfortable realities. Support for "pro-American" dictatorships such as Saudi Arabia and Egypt is not a Republican policy or a Democratic policy, it has been an American policy. All Americans have to bear the burden of maintaining or changing this policy.

The first American dilemma was resolved by implementing desegregation. How can the new global American dilemma be resolved? Even if the United States determined to resolve this new global dilemma, how could American foreign policy actually (and not just rhetorically) support the spread of democracy? In the final section, I suggest that the role of women is the key to bringing about this change.

AFTERWARD

The Veiled Solitude—Women as the Solution

Minoo is an energetic 26-year-old chemical engineer living in Tehran, Iran. Like all women in Iran, she is forced to wear the Islamic veil when she goes out in public. There is nothing she can do to escape what she calls the "imprisonment of the veil," but in many other ways she continues to try to work around the restrictions placed on women in the Islamic Republic. When she was in high school, she received a lot of advice about why it would not be a good idea for her to study engineering in university. "There are too many restrictions and taboos against women working as engineers," Minoo was told repeatedly.

"But there is no law against women studying engineering, so why should I place restrictions on myself? There are already too many restrictions on me as a woman, so why should I not take advantage of the few freedoms I do have?"

"Yes, you are free to study engineering according to the formal law of the land, but that does not mean that the men will actually let you work as an engineer," warned her mother.

"I will deal with that problem when I get to it, if I get to it," responded Minoo defiantly.

Unfortunately, it did not take long for Minoo to get to the problem of not being able to work as an engineer. Despite being an excellent engineer on paper, she never got the chance to practice her profession. Again and again she was told by potential employers that the job she had applied for required working in a situation where a woman would "not be able to cope." "We need an engineer who can sometimes work on the night shift in the factory," a factory manager told her, "How can a young unmarried woman do such a job? Besides, the men on the factory floor would not take you seriously." Another potential employer said, "We need someone who can travel to different parts of the country, how can a single woman be expected to do that? She would immediately attract the wrong kind of attention."

Minoo is one of many women in Iran and other major Muslim societies who have discovered that it is not enough to succeed in education. Well over half of undergraduates attending Iranian universities are females, but there are major obstacles in the larger society that still prevent women from developing their talents through work outside the home.

Hilal is a 17-year-old, high-school senior in Istanbul, Turkey. She is one of the top students in her school, being both an academic star and a natural leader among her group of friends, who are mostly practicing Muslims like her. Despite her outstanding grades, she was not certain that she would be going to university, not unless the Turkish government lifts a ban on women wearing headscarves at Turkish universities. Hilal strongly believes that women must cover their hair and dress in an "Islamic manner" when they go out in public.

Twenty-first-century elections in Turkey have entrenched the *Justice and Development Party*, and a "pro-Islamic" government with Recep Tayyip Erdogan as Prime Minister. This new "pro-Islamic" government is attempting to sweep aside restrictions placed on Islamic practices, such as the wearing of head scarves in universities, by Mustafa Kemal Atatürk (1881–1938), the father of modern Turkey and its first president (1923–1938). I visited Turkey as a child in the 1960s, and over the succeeding decades I have enjoyed a number of opportunities to revisit the country. It has been striking for me how more and more women active outside the home are wearing headscarves and there seems to be an "Islamic revival" in Turkey. Although the elite in Turkey still see the ideal future for their country as a "European" one, many young Turks now openly question the idea that their destiny is to be part of a secular, predominantly Christian Europe.

Turkey, Malaysia, Indonesia[1] . . . these are very large countries with predominantly Muslim populations and economies in a state of rapid change. In these countries there is, on the one hand, rapidly increasing numbers of university-educated women working outside the home and, on the other hand, a deep and sweeping revival of Islamic identity. These are countries in which it is not unusual to see women with professional higher degrees working as medical doctors, accountants, engineers, and university professors, also wearing the Islamic veil. The role of women seems to be changing in some important respects in these developing countries because the local economies need the talents of women.

The economies of Turkey, Malaysia, and Indonesia rely heavily on the large-scale participation of women in the labor force. This is very different from countries such as Saudi Arabia and Iran, where the national economy is almost exclusively reliant on wealth produced from the energy sector (oil and gas)—where a relatively small workforce of men can do all of the work to produce energy exports.

Zenab is 24 years old and lives with her upper middle-class family in Riyadh, Saudi Arabia. Although she achieved much better high-school grades than her two brothers, who were lazy and underperforming students, it was her brothers who were given the opportunity to travel to the West and spend time studying in England and the United States. After a lot of pleading with her family, Zenab was permitted to study at a local all-female higher education institution, in a Saudi "separate and unequal" education system that treats males and females very differently. Women in Saudi Arabia have severely limited roles outside the home and are not even permitted to drive cars. Zenab has never had problems with the "morality police" because she takes a lot of care to wear the Islamic veil as prescribed by law.

Arrangements have been made for Zenab to marry one of her relatives, and then she will begin to serve her only real role in the larger Saudi society: that of wife and mother. Her family is wealthy enough to employ servants and chauffeurs, and by hiring some workers who are English speaking, probably from the Indian subcontinent region, Zenab will at least be able to get some intellectual stimulation by practicing her English even after she gets married. She has pleaded with her father to allow her to work in the family business, but this avenue remains firmly closed to her. The real work in the family business is done by dozens of Indians and Pakistanis, and her family believes it would not be appropriate for a Saudi woman to interact with these foreign men.

Shareda is a 47-year-old graduate of a pioneering program for training Islamic chaplains at Hertford Seminary in Connecticut, United States. She is a Muslim with twenty years of service in the U.S. Army, almost four of them on active duty.[2] She is a second-generation immigrant; her parents, Trinidadians of Indian descent, moved from the Caribbean to the United States in 1972. Shareda has overcome many challenges, and she now faces the daunting task of becoming an Islamic chaplain in the U.S. Army.

The task is daunting because of two reasons. First, a Muslim chaplain would have the duty of leading Muslim soldiers in prayers, and in Islam it is men who always lead prayers. A woman could lead prayers only when other women are present, but not when men are present. Second, the U.S. military would find it very difficult to appoint a female Muslim chaplain as appointing such a chaplain would be seen as going against Islamic traditions. Indeed, the army has previously rejected Shareda's request on these grounds.

Shareda's plight is that the U.S. army, like other authorities in the West, has dared not attempt to implement policies based on a "reformed" Islam, even when the issue involves the implementation of "undemocratic" Islamic traditions and laws in western societies. There is no tradition of women serving as "Muslim ministers" in major Islamic societies, but such a tradition could be started in Islamic communities in the West. In order for this change to come about, authorities in the West need to take a stand in support of a more egalitarian role for women, including among Muslims. But the case of Shareda is important because it demonstrates that Muslim women come across obstacles toward equality even in the United States and other democracies.

Western politicians have repeatedly asserted that "moderate Muslims" need to take a stand against Islamic fundamentalism, but western governments and institutions have themselves failed to take such a stand. The case of Shareda is one of a very long line of examples, of failures by western governments to support a new liberated role for Muslim women. Consider, for example, the utter failure of western governments to take a strong stand against the *fatwa* issued against the author Salman Rushdie after the publication of his novel *The Satanic Verses* (1988). Instead of strongly supporting the principle of free speech and the rights of the author, western governments showed tepid support for the author. The result of this policy was Rushdie's book being taken off the shelves in some bookstores in major western cities, a move that further encouraged Islamic fanatics. In very much the same manner, the U.S. Army failed to strike out boldly and immediately accept Shareda's application to become a Muslim Chaplain. Rather, the Army went along with the traditional practice in Islamic communities of keeping women behind the men.

"Oil is a curse for us."

Several times during my childhood growing up in Tehran, Iran, I heard my mother commenting on the "oil curse." Over the decades, I have come to recognize the many ways in which oil has acted as a curse in Iran and in the other oil-producing countries of the Near and Middle East.

Most importantly, oil has been a curse because it has enabled a dictator and a small group of supporters to control an oil-producing country and remain immune from popular pressure. Experience shows that the oil-rich regimes that rule in Saudi Arabia and Iran are very difficult to overthrow because, as long as they control energy production, they can buy a military and security apparatus to keep the people under their thumbs. These "oil based" regimes do not depend on the people for income. The people of Iran could have opposed the Shah, which they did for many, many years, without having much impact, but what finally caused the Shah's downfall was the strike in the oil fields. When the oil stopped flowing, the fall of the Shah became inevitable.

The world powers, particularly the United States, have used the "oil curse" to their own advantage by putting into place and sustaining regimes that work in favor of American interests, such as the dictatorships of Saudi Arabia and Kuwait. The main function of such regimes is to guarantee a steady flow of cheap oil to the West through western oil companies. The 2003 invasion of Iraq continues this policy by enabling the United States a greater degree of control over Near and Middle East oil fields.

Of course, the "oil curse" can also backfire on the United States, in the new conditions of acute global energy shortage. In this new era, when an "anti-American" regime, such as the Ayatollahs in Iran or Chavez in Venezuela, comes to power, income from oil makes such a regime immune to pressure. Because the western powers need oil, and because China, India, and other fast-expanding countries provide alternative markets for oil, in the twenty-first century it is no longer viable to bring down anti-American regimes by imposing an oil embargo. Thus, oil not only makes dictators in Iran and other such countries impervious to pressure from their own populations, it also creates a strong buffer against attacks from the United States.

THE OIL CURSE AND WOMEN

The "oil curse" means that women can be excluded from public life in oil-producing countries such as Iran and Saudi Arabia, where only a relatively small group of men are needed to work in the process of oil production and exportation. A larger group of men are needed to work as part of a military and security apparatus in order to control the general population. The money for maintaining military and security forces comes from oil revenues. The regimes in oil-producing countries can survive without having taxes from the general population. Even if "the people" withhold taxes and go on strike, the regime will survive— as long as the oil fields are producing and oil exports continue and as long as the military and security apparatus receive large enough bribes to remain loyal to the regime.

In oil-producing countries, women can become very successful and overtake men in higher education, and still be excluded from participating in public life. This is simply because the dictatorships in countries such as Iran and Saudi Arabia, first, do not depend on income generated by women participating in the economy and, second, continue to treat women as second-class citizens in order to win the support of traditionalist males. Such traditionalist males fear that women, their wives, daughters, sisters, especially, will win freedom and escape their control. In these societies, women are the targets of displaced aggression—whenever the governments feel threatened, they crack down on so-called "immoral" behavior by women.[3]

The traditional assumption had been that women will inevitably gain equality through higher education, but this assumption has been shown to be wrong. Progress in education is one among a number of factors that will eventually help women gain freedom and equality in Islamic communities, but it is by no means sufficient by itself. In Islamic societies such as Turkey, Malaysia, and Indonesia women are making progress not just because of their success in higher education, but also because they are needed and being given a productive role in the larger economy. In these countries women can wear the veil and still be active and successful in the public arena. But, in countries under the influence of the "oil curse," women can be very successful in higher education and remain excluded from fruitful public life.

THE VEILED SOLITUDE

"You don't really understand!" Yasmeen asserted, "After all, the veil is just a piece of cloth. To wear the veil or not to wear the veil, it's of no consequence!"

I must admit I was puzzled. I had been sure that Yasmeen, a vibrant 22-year-old Pakistani university student, would be passionately against the veil. Yet, here she was exclaiming that the veil is "of no consequence."

"Do you really mean that you don't mind wearing the veil?" I asked.

"What I'm saying is that the veil is not the real issue. I can treat the veil like another piece of clothing I have to wear."

"So, what is the important issue?"

"It's what the veil has come to stand for, it's that the veil puts women in a solitude, at a distance from power, from the real action in public spaces."

"And what about women who say they wear the veil for protection?"

"Yes, the veil is protection from male threat—a threat that keeps us women in our solitude. From the time I was a little girl I was taught to fear men, to keep inside my solitude."

"But then why do you say that the veil is of no consequence?"

"Because...because what we really have to change is the role of women in the larger society, in public life, in the economy, in politics, in the law courts...did you know that women are not allowed to be judges in Islamic societies? And why? Because women are assumed to be incapable of making impartial judgments because women are supposed to be too emotional. Who starts the wars? Who does honor killings? It's the men of course! That really tells you who is emotional and incapable of making good judgments."

Three myths about national development have been shattered in the last half century. First, it is clear from the case of China and some other parts of the world that an open economy does not require or result in an open political system; freedom in the marketplace does not necessarily mean political freedom.[4] Second, it is clear from the situation of women in Pakistan and some other countries that just because a woman becomes head of a government and takes a leadership position such as prime-minister, it does not mean that the power and status of all women in that society will improve. Third, it is also clear from the case of Iran and some other countries that the success of women in higher education does not necessarily result in an improved situation for women, outside or even inside the home. Women can be highly educated but still be excluded from real power, both in the larger world and in the home.

Putting aside these myths, we can move to a more realistic approach to improving the situation of women in the Near and Middle East. What must also come about are changes in formal law so that women gain equal rights in business, political, family, and other major domains. An open economy, a female political leader, and better education for women, are all necessary, but not sufficient conditions for improving the situation of all women in Islamic communities. Changes in formal law are also necessary because such changes will help transform the Islamic family. The deeper motive for Islamic terrorism is to prevent changes in laws that transform the role of women in the family and the larger society.

The Islamic *hejab* has gained increasing importance internationally because it is symbolic of all the laws that keep women in their veiled solitude. Like other sacred carriers, the Islamic veil only has the meanings it is ascribed by us. All of us—including Islamic fundamentalists and reformers—have chosen to make the veil the line in the sand, the bunker behind which we make our stand. Islamic fundamentalists—in Basra and Baghdad, in Berlin, in Tehran, in London, in Riyadh, in Karachi, in Kuwait, in Cairo, in Istanbul, and in all the other centers where Muslims live—have taken up positions to defend the veil. Those who want to reform the Muslim world have taken up positions against the veil. But it may be that a fight over the veil can be sidestepped by reformers, it may be that the greater focus should be in changing laws and giving women more rights—from equal rights to drive cars on roads to equal rights to prevent their husbands from marrying additional wives and divorcing them and depriving them of their own children at will, from equal rights in business to equal rights in politics.

The reform of formal law in Islamic communities will eventually transform the Islamic family and have a profound impact on the larger Islamic world. Such changes will diminish the power of Islamic fundamentalists, resulting in decline and perhaps even extinction for radial Islamic movements. The evolutionary-developed instinct of Islamic fundamentalists has been to take defensive actions, such as terrorism. We should not expect these defensive actions to end soon. However, we can bring Islamic terrorism to an end sooner by facilitating the reform of formal law in Islamic communities, to give women equal rights, and to transform the Islamic family. Ultimately, the transformation of the role of women in the Islamic family will bring about the greatest revolution in Islamic communities.

NOTES

PREFACE

1. Theodore Levitt (1925–2006), a Harvard business professor, is credited with having coined the term globalization. Giddens (2000), Reich (2007), Cohen (2006) and Cowen (2002) are among the most insightful authors who have examined the enormous economic and cultural changes accompanying globalization. Their analyses suggest that we are truly entering a new era, with vast economic and cultural changes taking place that are to a large extent out of the control of individual nation states, or even powerful regional units such as the European Union.

2. For more on the idea of identity barriers and identity threat as being associated with terrorism, see Moghaddam (2006), as well as various authors in Rothbart and Korostelina (2006).

3. See Bello, *Deglobalization* (2002), p. xii.

CHAPTER 1

1. Dabashi (2007) and Gheissari (2006) both provide useful and well-written examinations of developments in contemporary Iran with some historical context.

2. I borrow this phrase from the highly insightful work of Arjomand, *The Turban for the Crown* (1988).

3. Tehran is now one of the most overcrowded, polluted, and expensive cities in the world. The population of Greater Tehran is about 20 million, and in 2008 property prices in northern Tehran are comparable to New York and London.

4. There is often confusion in the West about what "Hezbollah" means. In Lebanon, Hezbollah is a social-military organization with a formal hierarchical

structure, active in "military defense of Muslims," but also providing educational and health services. The Lebanese Hezbollah has been branded a terrorist organization by the U.S. government and has a history of fighting the Israeli military. Indeed, Hezbollah claims to have driven the Israeli military out of southern Lebanon. In Iran, on the other hand, the term Hezbollah simply refers to individuals who are Islamic fundamentalists and support fundamentalist political causes. Although such individuals may belong to organizations such as the Islamic Guards or the "Baseej," there is not in Iran a formal organization termed Hezbollah. For a discussion of the link between Iran and Hezbollah in the Near and Middle East context, see Grace (2006).

5. There is a strong case for asserting that religious fundamentalists share certain basis psychological characteristics; see Hood (2005) and Herriot (2007) for more indepth discussions.

6. Practicing Muslims interpret the Koran in line with the demands of modern societies and are to some extent open to influence from the West, whereas fundamentalist Muslims demand a return to "pure" Islam as they imagine it was practiced in days of the Prophet Mohammad and attempt to shut out western influence.

7. Fundamentalists are at the deeper level enemies of freedom, although their surface ideology can take many forms, including communism, capitalism, Muslim, Jewish, Christian, and so on. There is a rich literature on such "true believers" (Hoffer, 2002), although much of academic research has focused on their right-wing authoritarian tendencies (Altemeyer 1988) and neglected left-wing enemies of freedom.

8. Khomeini became a *marja-i-taqlid* (source of imitation) among Shi'a Muslim fundamentalists from the 1960s. He was already a leading theologian at the *howzeh elmieh Ghom* when he clashed with the Shah of Iran and was sent into exile to Turkey, Iraq, and France from 1964. For a sampling of his ideas, see Khomeini (2002).

9. See Ishiguro, *The Remains of the Day* (1988).

10. See Conason, 2008

11. See the discussions of different globalizations in Berger and Huntington, 2002. Appadurai (1996) has noted that "Globalization does not necessarily or even frequently imply homogenization or Americanization..." (p. 17). There has been too little attention to globalization from non-western psychologists, although western psychologists have started to examine the psychological aspects of globalization (Arnett, 2002; Hermans and Kempen, 1998).

12. The thorny issue of language policy and diversity in the United States is reviewed by Crawford (2000).

13. Robertson (1992) has written with keen insight about the challenges of cultural and identity coherence confronting different peoples as globalization pushed groups into contact with "strangers."

14. I am not suggesting that all non-western societies have the exactly the same experience with globalization in every way. Globalization is bringing with

it new perceived threats in relations between non-western societies and some of these are unique to particular countries—an example being the threat Japan perceives as a result of the emergence of China as a world economic power. The Japanese are alarmed that their ancient regional rival is predicted to overtake them.

15. The concept of ethnocentrism has a long history in the social sciences, going back at least to Sumner's 1906 discussion "Loyalty to the group, sacrifice for it, hatred and contempt for outsiders, brotherhood within, warlikeness without..." (p. 12). LeVine and Campbell (1972) provide an extensive cross-cultural review of ethnocentrism.

16. There is a long history of humanitarian authors, such as Sir Thomas More (1478–1535), being enthusiastic about a one-world "utopia."

17. The explosions arising from fractured globalization could shake off the "veil" of modern nation states that western powers imposed on the Near and Middle East in the twentieth century. In Iraq, the Kurdish north and the Shi'a south are moving independently away from the Sunni Arab center. In Pakistan, Baluch, Pashtun, and Sindhi minorities are no longer being controlled by the Punjabi majority, and parts of the country are out of the control of the central government.

18. *Freedom House*, which tracks global trends in political freedoms, has been optimistic in its assessments of the march of democracy (in line with publicity about the "freedom agenda" of the White House during the presidency of George W. Bush (2000–2008). A more realistic assessment and *Democracy Index* were put forward by *The Economist* in 2007, showing a definite halt to the spread of democracy at the start of the twenty-first century.

19. The concept of carriers is introduced in Moghaddam (2002).

20. The rivalry between Sunni and Shi's and the recent "Shi's revival" is discussed in Nasre (2006).

21. According to Dell'Orto (2008), the American dream has been particularly strong in Europe, but has become shaken in the early twenty-first century.

22. The belief that terrorists are pathological is still widely held, despite the evidence to the contrary, see Ruby (2002). A few exceptional cases have been reported. For example, on Feb 1, 2008, two female suicide bombers who killed nearly 100 people in Baghdad, had records of psychiatric illness, supposedly schizophrenia (as reported by Oppel, 2008).

23. In this discussion I am not concerned with the question of "who I am." I can know "who I am" by looking at my driving license or passport.

24. It is in the realm of collective behavior and group and intergroup dynamics that Freud shows his true genius, see particularly Freud (1955, 1957).

25. The importance of the family in shaping behavior has been underestimated, but there is a gradual turn to give more importance to the family in mental health. These changes are to some extent rooted in the radical views of the Scottish psychiatrist Ronald D. Laing (1927–1989) about the impact of the family on personal development.

PART I

1. The Second Coming, p. 99.
2. Trilling, *Sincerity and Authenticity* (1971), p. 1.
3. The growing economic power of the expanded European Union, China, and India, suggests that these will join Russia and the United States as power centers in the first half of the twenty-first century.

CHAPTER 2

1. Zimbardo (2007) presents a brilliant assessment of the culpability of Rumsfeld and others in the 2000–2008 Bush administration.
2. See Moghaddam (2007) for a fuller discussion of the deeper psychological reasons why torture is carried out; reasons that have nothing to do with information gathering.
3. Winter (2003) provides a very useful discussion of the conditions in which personality becomes more important in political contexts.
4. For a more extensive discussion of the concept of personality and psychological measures of personality traits, see Moghaddam (2005, ch. 13).
5. The relationship between identification and degrees of freedom has many different aspects, and in this discussion I am only concerned with identification strength and conformity. For broader treatment of the role of identification in collective processes, see the discussions in Postmes and Jetten (2006).
6. The concepts of performance capacity and performance style are discussed in a more indepth manner in Moghaddam (2002).
7. For a review of the research literature in this area, see Moghaddam (2005, chapters 15 and 16).
8. For an excellent discussion of how modern psychology came into being, see Danziger (1990).
9. See the discussion of long-term potentiation in chapter 5 and of artificial intelligence in chapter 8 of Moghaddam (2005).
10. For more details, see Chapter 5 in Moghaddam, *Multiculturalism and Intergroup Relations* (2008).
11. Palmer and Palmer (2002) provide a well-written review of evolutionary psychology.
12. First published in 1976, *The Selfish Gene* was published in revised form most recently in 2006.
13. Social identity theory and the role of identity in intergroup relations are discussed further in Moghaddam, *Multiculturalism and Intergroup Relations* (2008), ch. 4.
14. An account of the behaviorist tradition and a list of further reading are provided in Chapter 6 of Moghaddam (2005).
15. Thoreau, *Walden and Civil Disobedience* (1854/2003), p. 74.
16. Skinner (1948/1976 , p. 93).
17. Skinner, *Beyond Freedom and Dignity* (1971).

18. Skinner, *Walden Two* (1948/1976), p. x.

19. For a more extensive discussion of social constructionism, see Danziger (1997) and chapter 20 in Moghaddam (2005).

20. The role and status of women in the Indian subcontinent is paradoxical in some ways. Although India, Pakistan, and Sri Lanka have had women as national political leaders, the situation of most women in everyday life in these countries is far from equal and fair. Men continue to have higher power and status in interpersonal and family relations.

21. Goldstein, *Natural History* (1987), p. 109.

22. Childs, *History of the Family* (2003).

CHAPTER 3

1. Ehrlich, *Human Natures: Genes, Cultures, and the Human Prospect* (2000).

2. Moghaddam, *The Individual and Society* (2002), p.40.

3. Donne (1623/1975)

4. Dostoyevsky, *Crime and Punishment* (1866/1951), p. 542.

5. The nature of the "distinctiveness motive" is explored in a number of empirical studies and is the topic of interesting theorizing, see Brewer, *Personality and Social Psychology Bulletin* (1991) and Lee, Lessem & Moghaddam in, *Global Conflict Resolution Through Positioning Analysis* (2007).

6. For further discussions of conformity, see chapter 7 in Moghaddam *Social Psychology* (1998) and chapter 15 in Moghaddam, *Great Ideas in Psychology* (2005).

7. See Hobbes, *Leviathan* (1651/1991).

8. See Locke, *Social Contract* (1690/1948).

9. See Hume, *Social Contract* (1748/1948).

10. See Rousseau, *The Social Contract and Other Later Political Writings* (1762/1997).

11. Gough (1963) provides an insightful critical discussion of what I have termed the "classical" social contract.

12. Indeed, fairness rules seem to influence animals as well as humans, see Bekoff, *Wild Justice and Fair Play* (2005) and Bekoff, Allen & Burghardt, *The Cognitive Animal* (2002).

13. See Esposito and Mogahed, *Who speaks for Islam?* (2008).

14. Tolstoy, *War and Peace* (1869/1957), vol.1, p. 455.

15. For a more indepth discussion of illusions of control, see Moghaddam and Studer, *Illusions of Control* (1998).

16. Runciman, *Relative Deprivation and Social Justice* (1966).

17. Janeway, *Immunobiology* (1999).

18. Agrawal and Agrawal, *Environmental Pollution and Plant Response* (1999).

19. McCarthy and Campbell, *Security Transformation* (2001).

CHAPTER 4

1. Sherif, *Group Conflict and Cooperation* (1966).

2. For further discussion of these shared human characteristics, see Moghaddam, *Social Psychology* (1998/2002).

3. The classic research on this is reported by Martin and Clark (1987).

4. From among Marx's very extensive writings, the most accessible and relevant are Marx, *Collected Works of Karl Marx and Frederick Engels* (1852/1979) and Marx and Engels, *Communist Manifesto* (1848/1967).

5. See Bouillon, *Libertarians and Liberalism* (1996). For a recently influential capitalist version of historical development, see Fukuyama (1992, 2006).

6. Tolstoy, 1985

7. Popper, The open society and its enemies (1966).

8. Sidanius and Pratto, *Social Dominance* (1999).

9. Zangwill *The Melting Pot* (1909).

10. Allport, *The Nature of Prejudice* (1954).

11. Crystal, *Language Death* (2000).

12. Berscheid and Reis (1998).

13. Schneider, Smith, Taylor, and Fleener, *Personality and Organizations* (1998).

14. For example, see Hymes, Leinart, Rowe, and Rogers, *Journal of Applied Psychology* (1993).

15. Osbeck, Moghaddam, and Perreault, *International Journal of Intercultural Relations* (1977).

16. For example, see arguments presented in Stephens, *The Idea of Democracy* (1993), and Welsh, *Ethnic Conflict and International Security* (1993).

17. The concept of cultural literacy is discussed in Hirsch, *Cultural Literacy* (1988).

18. By 2003, among United States citizens more women than men earned doctorates, see Smallwood, *Chronicle of Higher Education* (2003).

19. See Moghaddam, *Multiculturalism and Intergroup Relations* (2008), p. 128.

CHAPTER 5

1. Yeats, *W.B. Yeats Selected Poetry* (1962).

2. Bello, *Deglobalization* (2002).

3. Homer-Dixon, *The Upside of Down* (2006), p. 186–187.

4. Johnston, tax data from 2005 shows the greatest U.S. income inequality since the depression (2007).

5. Marmot, *The Status Syndrome* (2004).

6. See Meyer and Geschiere (1999) for a discussion of globalization and identity development.

7. Smith, *An Inquiry into the Nature and Causes of the Wealth of Nations* (1776/1976).

8. Ritzer, *McDonaldization* (2006).

9. For an example new regionalism discussions, see Wong, *Indicators for Urban and Regional Planning* (2006).

10. Moghaddam, *Religion and Regional Planning: The Case of the Emerging "Shi'a Region"* (in press).

11. Caporael, *Individuals Self, Relational Self, Collective Self* (2001), p. 255.

12. Eible-Eibesfeldt, *Human Ethology* (1989), p.100.

13. Emlen, *An Evolutionary Theory of the Family* (1995).

14. For further discussion, see Moghaddam, *The Changing Canadian Metropolis* (1994).

15. An outcome of this work was Moghaddam and Studer, *Illusions of Control* (1998).

16. Sageman (2004, 2007) has accumulated impressive evidence suggesting that individuals are often pulled into terrorist networks through social affiliation needs.

17. Peter Mandaville and Marc Sageman are among the authors who have discussed terrorism in the age of globalization, see Mandaville, *Global Political Islam* (2007) and Sageman, *Leaderless Jihad* (2007).

18. For a more indepth discussion of specialization and its consequences, see Moghaddam, *The Specialized Society* (1997).

19. Reported by Landler in *The New York Times* (2007), p. A10.

20. Reported by Smith in *The New York Times* (2007), p. A10.

21. Reported by Burns in *The New York Times* (2008).

22. Reported by Nugent and Menuhin in *The Times* (2007), p. 8.

23. Bowen, *Why the French Don't Like Headscarves* (2006).

24. Reported by Perlez in *The New York Times* (2007), p. A.1.

25. Myers and Kent, *The New Consumers* (2004).

26. In *Putin* (2008), Sakwa provides a well-written description of Putin and the new Russian elite.

27. Machine breaking by the Luddites is discussed in Thomis, *The Luddites* (1970).

PART II

1. The processes of Europeanization and efforts to bring about cohesion in these processes is discussed by Bache, *Europeanization and Multilevel Government* (2008).

2. See Pyszczynski, Solomon, and Greenberg, *In the Wake of 9/11* (2003). According to this new theory "Terror management is posited to be an unconscious and ongoing defense that serves to avert the potential for terror engendered by the knowledge of mortality" (p. 55).

CHAPTER 6

1. Darwin *The Origin of Species by Means of Natural Selection* (1859/1993), pp. 385–386.

2. Catastrophic evolution and related concepts are first discussed in Moghaddam (2006).

3. Hewstone and Brown, *Contact and Conflict in Intergroup Encounters* (1986).

4. Pettigrew and Tropp, *A Meta-Analytical Test of Intergroup Contact Theory* (2006).

5. Venter et al., The Sequence of the Human Genome (2001).

6. Myers and Kent, *The New Consumers* (2004, p. 3).

7. Cavalli-Sforza, Menozzi and Piazza, *The History and Geography of Human Genes* (1994).

8. Wells, *The Journey of Man* (2002).

9. Baskin, *A Plague of Rats and Rubber Vines* (2002).

10. Ruiz and Carlton, *Invasive Species* (2004).

11. On February 13, 2008, Prime Minister Kevin Rudd of Australia changed direction by offering a formal apology to Aborigines for their mistreatment, including policies designed to "breed out the color."

12. For example, see Chagnon's (1997) indepth study of the Yanomamo. Although Chagnon has been criticized on ethical grounds for some of his assumed practices in the field, I believe his basic findings are of great value.

13. Hart, Pilling and Goodale *The Tiwi of Northern Australia* (2001).

14. For example, see Mann, *New Revelations of the Americas Before Columbus* (2006).

15. Josephy, *The Indian Heritage of America* (1991).

16. Reader, *Africa* (1998).

17. Ryan, *The Aboriginal Tasmanians* (1981).

18. Turnbull, *The Mountain People* (1972).

19. Crystal, *Language Death* (2000) and Nettle and Romaine, *Vanishing Voices* (2000) provide excellent but unsettling reviews of the vanishing of languages around the world.

20. Dalby, *Language in Danger* (2003).

CHAPTER 7

1. Vick, *Iran's Khatami Says Islam Is the Enemy West Needs* (2006, p. A17).

2. Masood, Pakistan's Violent Protests over Cartoons Taking Political Turn (2006).

3. Cowell, *Islamic Schools Test Ideal of Integration in Britain* (2006).

4. Crocker and Major, *Social Stigma and Self-Esteem* (1989).

5. Mearsheimer and Walt, *The Israeli Lobby and U.S. Foreign Policy* (2007).

6. Moghaddam, *From the Terrorists' Point of View* (2006).

7. See the discussion in Chapter 9 of Moghaddam, *Great Ideas in Psychology* (2005).

8. Taylor, *The Quest for Identity* (2002), p. 41.

9. Moghaddam, *Interobjectivity and Culture* (2003).

10. Waxman, *"Pirates" Haul So Far Estimated at $401 Million* (2007).

11. For a discussion of the concept of change as it relates to human behavior, see Moghaddam, *The Individual and Society* (2002).

12. Moghaddam, *The Specialized Society* (1997).

13. Evidence for this can be found in data produced by the *Eurobarometer* project, http://europa.eu.int/comm/public_opinion/index_en.htm, through which public opinion among the European Union population is regularly assessed. In general, identification with country is stronger than identification with Europe, just as pride in country is higher than pride in Europe. Also, participation rate in European elections is lower than in national elections.

14. Frank and Cook, *The Winner-Takes-All Society* (1995).

15. Esposito and Mogahed, *Who Speaks for Islam?* (2008).

CHAPTER 8

1. Huntington, *The Clash of Civilization and the Remaking of World Order* (1996), particularly pages 70–71.

2. Ibid., p. 193.

3. Glendon (2001) provides an excellent account of Elenor Roosevelt's pivotal role in the shaping of the United Nations Declaration of Human Rights.

4. For example, see the critical approach of John Bolton (2007), President George W. Bush's choice for ambassador to the United Nations and a leader of right-wing ideologues in the area of foreign policy.

5. Louis and Taylor, *The Psychology of Rights and Duties* (2004), p. 105.

6. This is reflected in a substantial literature on "comparative legal cultures." For example, New York University Press has published a series of books under the general topic of "legal cultures," an example being Varga (1992), which includes a good range of discussions about different legal cultures.

7. Putnam, *Bowling Alone* (2000).

8. For a more extensive consideration of rights and duties across cultures, see the readings in Finkel and Moghaddam (2005).

9. Glaberson, *U.S. Asks Court to Limit lawyers at Guantánamo* (2007).

10. Greg Behrman (2007) has convincingly argued that *The Marshall Plan,* although "noble," is very difficult to replicate.

11. The term "sociobiology" is seen to have become too controversial and has been abandoned, because of its supposed links with eugenics (the plan to "breed better humans") and other dangerous ideas. Most researchers now use the term "evolutionary psychology," which is discussed in chapter 19 of Moghaddam (2005).

12. Examples of research demonstrating a sense of fairness in animals are found in Bekoff (2005), Bekoff, Allen, and Burghardt (2002), and Brosnan and de Waal (2003).

13. Langford et al., *Social Modulation of Pain As Evidence for Empathy in Mice* (2006).

14. A case for the presence of an inbuilt "moral grammar" is discussed in Hauser (2006).

15. Writing about the case of Sami Al-Hajj, an Al Jazeera cameraman, who was been on hunger strike to protest his mistreatment at Guantánamo Bay Prison, Nicjolar Kristof (2008) points out that "Mr. Hajj's fortitude has turned him into a household name in the Arab world, and his story is sowing anger at the authorities holding him without trial. That's us."

PART III

1. Moghaddam, *From the Terrorists' Point of View* (2006).
2. As discussed in chapter 6 in Moghaddam, *Multiculturalism and Intergroup Relations* (2008) and Moghaddam and Riley, *The Psychology of Rights and Duties* (2005).
3. Moghaddam, *From the Terrorists' Point of View* (2006).

CHAPTER 9

1. Myrdal, *An American Dilemma* (1944).
2. Ibid., p. 4.
3. Hamilton, Madison, and Jay, *The Federalist Papers* (1996).
4. See Festinger, *A Theory of Cognitive Dissonance* (1957).
5. Egan, Santos, and Bloom, *The Origins of Cognitive Dissonance* (2007).
6. See Neimann and Maruyama, Inequalities in higher education (2005).
7. See Moghaddam, *Multiculturalism and Intergroup Relations* (2008), pp. 105–106).
8. Lehecka and Delbanco, *Ivy-league Let Down* (2008), p. A 21.
9. Ehrenreich, *Nickel and Dimed* (2002).
10. This would be taken by left-wing analysts as reflecting false consciousness, with a less powerful group adopting the ideology of the more powerful group, even when that ideology best serves the interests of the existing power elites (Marx 1979/1852; Marx & Engels, 1848/1967).
11. Jost and Banaji, *The Role of Stereotyping in System Justification and the Production of False consciousness* (1994).
12. Dowd, *Faith, Freedom and Bling in the Middle East* (2008), p. A 23.
13. Myers and Kent, *The New Consumers* (2004).
14. The State of the Union Address as reported in *The New York Times*, Jan 29, 2008, p. A18.
15. Altemeyer, *Enemies of Freedom* (1988).
16. Cooper, *White House Criticizes Envoy over Iran* (2008).
17. Shanker and Fathi, Iran shows its own video of vessels' encounter in Gulf (2008a).
18. Shanker and Knowlton, Iranian boats confront U.S. in Persian Gulf (2008b), p. A4.
19. Moghaddam and Kavulich, *The Cambridge Handbook of Sociocultural Psychology* (2007); *Global Conflict Resolution through Positioning Analysis* (2008).

20. See Moghaddam, *Interrogation Policy and American Psychology in Global Context* (2007).

21. Echebarria-Echabe and Fernández-Guede, *Effects of Terrorism on Attitudes and ideological orientation* (2006).

22. See "The words that were used," in *The New York Times*, Jan 29, 2008, p. A18.

23. Huddy, Khatib and Capelos, *Reactions to Terrorist Attacks of September 11, 2001* (2002).

24. Oswald (2006).

AFTERWARD

1. Indonesia has by far the largest population among Muslim nations, and is seen as a stabilizing factor in Southeast Asia. However, the Bali bombings that killed about 200 people in 2002 and other more recent terrorist attacks lend support to the view that Al Qaeda inspired groups and Islamic separatists have become ideologically and tactically connected in Indonesia.

2. Murphy (2008).

3. The victimization of women is part of a larger irrational and destructive set of behaviors particularly characteristic of the Near and Middle East. The author Philip Winslow captured this in his discussion of how in the West Bank, "victory for us is to see you suffer" (see Winslow, 2007).

4. I would agree that the lack of political openness results in corruption in the business domain, and the Chinese economy is hampered by corruption. Many commentators have overlooked this fact, and exaggerated the growth potential of China. Just as the prospects of Japan becoming "number 1" in the world were grossly exaggerated in the 1970s and 1980s, the growth potential of China is being exaggerated in the 21st century.

REFERENCES

Agrawal, S.B. and Agrawal, M. (Eds.) (1999). *Environmental Pollution and Plant Response*. Boca Raton, FL: Lewis Publishers.

Allport, G.W. (1954). *The Nature of Prejudice*. Cambridge, MA: Addison-Wesley.

Altemeyer, B. (1988). *Enemies of Freedom: Understanding Right-Wing Authoritarianism*. San Francisco, CA: Jossey-Bass.

Appadurai, A. (1996). *Modernity At Large: Cultural Dimensions of Globalization*. Minneapolis, MN: University of Minnesota Press.

Arjomand, A.A. (1988). *The Turban for the Crown*. New York: Oxford University Press.

Arnett, J.J. (2002). The psychology of globalization. *American Psychologist, 57*, 774–783.

Bache, I. (2008). *Europeanization and Multilevel Government: Cohesion Policy in the European Union and Britain*. Lanham: Rowman & Littlefield.

Baskin, Y. (2002). *A Plague of Rats and Rubber Vines*. Washington, DC: Island Press.

Bekoff, M. (2005). *Wild Justice and Fair Play: Cooperation, Forgiveness, and Morality in Animals*. Chicago, IL: University of Chicago Press.

Bekoff, M., Allen, C., and Burghardt, G.M. (Eds.) (2002). *The Cognitive Animal*. Cambridge, MA: MIT Press.

Bello, W. (2002). *Deglobalization: Ideas for a New World Economy*. New updated edition. London, UK: Zed Books.

Berger, P.L. and Huntington, S.P. (Eds.) (2002). *Many Globalizations: Cultural Diversity in the Contemporary World*. New York: Oxford University Press.

Berham, G. (2007). *The Most Noble Adventure*. New York: Free Press.

Berscheid, E., and Reis, H.T. (1998). Attraction and close relationship. In D.T. Gilbert, S.T. Fiske & G. Lindzey (Eds.), *The Handbook of Social Psychology* (4th ed., pp. 193–281). New York: McGrow–Hill.

Bolten, J. (2007). *Surrender Is Not an Option: Defending America at the United Nations and Abroad.* New York: Threshold.

Bouillon, H. (Ed.) (1996). *Libertarians and Liberalism.* Aldershot, Hants, UK: Avebury.

Bowen, J.R. (2006). *Why the French Don't Like Headscarves.* Princeton, NJ: Princeton University Press.

Brewer, M. (1991). The social self: On being the same and different at the same time. *Personality and Social Psychology Bulletin, 17,* 475–482.

Brosnan, S.F. and de Waal, F.B.M. (2003). Monkeys reject unequal pay. *Nature, 425,* 297–299.

Burns, J.F. (2008). Top Anglicans rally to besieged archbishop. *The New York Times,* Feb.12, p. A7.

Canason, J. (2008). *It Can Happen Here: Authoritarian Peril in the Age of Bush.* New York: St. Martin's Press.

Caporael, L.R. (2001). Parts and wholes: The evolutionary importance of groups. In C. Sedikides and M.B. Brewer (Eds.), *Individuals Self, Relational Self, Collective Self.* Philadelphia, PA: Psychology Press.

Cavalli-Sforza, L., Menozza, P., and Piazza, A. (1994). *The History and Geography of Human Genes.* Princeton, NJ: Princeton University Press.

Chagnon, N.A. (1997). *Yanomamo.* (5th ed.). New York: Harcourt Brace.

Childs, G. (2003). Polyandry and population growth in a historical Tibetan society. *History of the Family, 8,* 423–444.

Cohen, D. (2006). *Globalization and Its Enemies.* (Translated by J. B. Baker). Cambridge, MA.: MIT Press.

Conason, J. (2007). *It Could Happen Here: Authoritarian Peril in the Age of Bush.* New York: Thomas Dunne Books.

Cooper, H. (2008). White House criticizes envoy over Iran. *The New York Times,* January 30, p. A9.

Cowell, A. (2006). Islamic schools test ideal of integration in Britain. *The New York Times,* October 15, p. 12.

Cowen, T. (2002). *Creative Destruction: How Globalization is Changing the World's Cultures.* Princeton, NJ: Princeton University Press.

Crawford, J. (2000). *At War with Diversity: US Language Policy in an Age of Anxiety.* Buffalo, NY: Multilingual Matters.

Crocker, J. and Major, B. (1989). Social stigma and self-esteem: The self-protective properties of stigma. *Psychological Review, 96,* 608–630.

Crystal, D. (2000). *Language Death.* Cambridge, UK: Cambridge University Press.

Dabashi, H. (2007). *Iran: A People Interrupted.* New York: Free Press.

Dalby, A. (2003). *Language in Danger: The Loss of Linguistic Diversity and the Threat to Our Future.* New York: Columbia University Press.

Danziger, K. (1990). *Constructing the Subject: Historical Origins of Psychological Research.* Cambridge, UK: Cambridge University Press.

Danziger, K. (1997). The varieties of social constructionism. *Theory and Psychology*, 7, 399–416.

Darwin, C. (1859/1993). *The Origin of Species by Means of Natural Selection or the Preservation of Favored Races in the Struggle for Life*. New York: The Modern Library.

Dawkins, R. (2006). *The Selfish Gene*. Oxford, UK: Oxford University Press.

Dell'Orto, G. (2008). *The Hidden Power of the American Dream: Why Europe's Shaken Confidence in the United States Threatens the Future of U.S. Influence*. Westport, CT: Praeger Security International.

Donne, J. (1623/1975). *Devotions upon Emergent Occasions* (Ed. A. Raspa). Montreal: McGill University Press.

Dostoyevsky, F.M. (1866/1951). *Crime and Punishment*. (D. Magarshack, translator). Harmonsworth, Middlesex: Penguin Classics.

Dowd, M. (2008). Faith, freedom and bling in the Middle East. *The New York Times*, January 16, p. A23.

Echebarria-Echabe, A. and Fernández-Guede, E. (2006). Effects of terrorism on attitudes and ideological orientation. *European Journal of Social Psychology*, 26, 259–265.

Ehrenreich, B. (2002). *Nickel and Dimed: On (Not) Getting by in America*. New York: Holt.

Ehrlich, P.R. (2000). *Human Natures: Genes, Cultures, and the Human Prospect*. Washington, DC: Shearwater.

Eibl-Eibesfeldt, I. (1989). *Human Ethology*. New York: Aldine de Gruyter.

Egan, L.C., Santos, L.R., and Bloom, P. (2007). The Origins of Cognitive Dissonance. *Psychological Science*, 18, 978–983.

Emlen, S.T. (1995). An evolutionary theory of the family. *Proceedings of the National Academy of Sciences of the United States of America*, 92, 8092–8099.

Esposito, J.L., and Mogahed, D. (2008). *Who Speaks for Islam? What a Bullion Muslims Really Think*. Washington, DC: Gallup Press.

Festinger, L. (1957). *A Theory of Cognitive Dissonance*. Stanford, CA: Stanford University Press.

Finkel, N. and Moghaddam, F.M. (Eds.) (2005). *The Psychology of Rights and Duties: Empirical Contributions and Normative Commentaries*. Washington, DC: American Psychological Association Press.

Frank, R., and Cook, P. (1995). *The Winner-Takes-All Society*. New York: Simon & Schister.

Freud, S. (1955). Group psychology and the analysis of the ego. In J. Strachy (Ed. and Trans.), *The Standard Edition of the Complete Psychological Works of Sigmund Freud* (Vol. 18, pp. 67–143). London: Hogarth Press. (Original work published in 1921.)

Freud, S. (1957). Thoughts for the times on war and death. In J. Strachy (Ed. and Trans.), *The Standard Edition of the Complete Psychological Works of Sigmund Freud* (Vol. 14, pp. 271–302). London: Hogarth Press. (Original work published in 1915.)

Fukuyama, F. (1992). *The End of History and the Last Man*. New York: Free Press.

Fukuyama, F. (2006). Democracy and "The End of History" revisited. In H. Muñoz (Ed.), *Democracy Rising: Assessing the Global Challenges* (pp. 115–120). Boulder, CO: Lynne Rienner.

Gheissari, A. (2006). *Democracy in Iran: History and Quest for Liberty*. New York: Oxford University Press.

Giddens, A. (2000). *Runaway World: How Globalization Is Reshaping Our Lives*. New York: Routledge.

Glaberson, W. (2007). U.S. asks court to limit lawyers at Guantánamo. *The New York Times*, April 26, pp. A1 and A20.

Glendon, M.A. (2001). *A World Made New: Elenor Roosevelt and the United Nations Declaration of Human Rights*. New York: Random House.

Goldstein, M.C. (1987). When brothers share a wife. *Natural History*, 96, 109–112.

Gough, J.W. (1963. *The Social Contract*. 2nd ed. London: Oxford University Press.

Grace, R. (2006). *Understanding the Iran-Hezbollah Connection*. Washington, DC: United States Institute of Peace.

Hamilton, A., Madison, J., and Jay, J. (1996). *The Federalist Papers* (B.F. Wright, Ed.). New York: Barnes & Noble. (Original work published in 1787–1788.)

Hart, C.W.M., Pilling, A.R., and Goodale, J.C. (2001). *The Tiwi of Northern Australia* (3rd.ed.). Belmont, CA: Wadsworth/Thompson Learning.

Hauser, M.D. (2006). *Moral Minds*. New York: HarperCollins.

Hermans, H.J.M. and Dimaggio, G. (2007). Self, identity, and globalization in times of uncertainty: A dialogical analysis. *Review of General Psychology*, 11, 31–61.

Hermans, H.J.M. and Kempen, H.J.G. (1998). Moving cultures: The perilous problems of cultural dichotomies in a globalizing society. *American Psychologist*, 53, 1111–1120.

Herriot, P. (2007). *Religious Fundamentalism and Social Identity*. London: Routledge.

Hewstone, M. and Brown, R.J. (1986). Contact is not enough: An intergroup perspective on the contact hypothesis. In M. Hewstone and R.J. Brown (Eds.), *Contact and Conflict in Intergroup Encounters* (pp. 3–44). Oxford, UK: Blackwell.

Hirsch, E.D. Jr. (1988). *Cultural Literacy: What Every American Needs to Know*. New York: Viking Books.

Hobbes, T. (1651/1948). *Leviathan*. (Ed. R. Tuck). Cambridge, UK: Cambridge University Press.

Hoffer, E. (2002). *The True Believer: Thoughts on the Nature of Mass Movements*. New York: Perennial.

Homer-Dixon, T. (2006). *The Upside of Down: Catastrophe, Creativity, and the Renewal of Civilization*. Washington, DC: Island Press.

Hood, R.W. (2005). *The Psychology of Religious Fundamentalism*. New York: Guilford Press.

Huddy, L., Khatib, N., and Capelos, T. (2002). Reactions to terrorist attacks of September 11, 2001. *Public Opinion Quarterly*, 66, 418–415.

Hume, D. (1748/1948). Of the original contract. In E. Barker (Ed.), *Social Contract Essays by Locke, Hume and Rousseau* (pp. 147–166). London, UK: Oxford University Press.

Huntington, S. (1996). *The Clash of Civilization and the Remaking of World Order*. New York: Touchstone.

Hymes, R.W., Leinart, M., Rowe, S., and Rogers, W. (1993). Acquaintance rape: The effect of race of defendant and race of victim on white juror decisions. *Journal of Social Psychology, 133*, 627–634.

Ishiguro, K. (1988). *The Remains of the Day*. New York: Vintage International.

Janeway, C.A. et al (1999). *Immunobiology: The Immune System in Health and Disease*. London, UK: Garland Publishing.

Johnston, D.C. (2007). Tax data from 2005 shows the greatest U.S. income inequality since the depression. *The New York Times*, March 29, pp.C1 and C10.

Josephy, A.M., Jr. (1991). *The Indian Heritage of America*. Boston, MA: Houghton-Mifflin.

Jost, J.T. and Banaji, M.R. (1994). The role of stereotyping in system justification and the production of false consciousness. *British Journal of Social Psychology, 33*, 1–27.

Khomeini, R. (2002). *Islam and Revolution: The Writings and Declaration of Imam Khomeini*. New York: Kegan Paul.

Kristof, N.D. (2008). When we torture. *The New York Times*, Feb. 14, p. A.31.

Landler, M. (2007). German judge cites Koran, stirring up cultural storm. *The New York Times*, March 23, p. A10.

Langford, D.J., Crager, S.E., Shehzad, Z., Smith, S.B., Sotocinal, S.G., Levenstadt, J.S., et al (2006, June 30). Social modulation of pain as evidence for empathy in mice. *Science, 312*, 1967–1970.

Lee, N., Lessem, E., and Moghaddam, F.M. (2007). Standing out and blending in: Differentiation and conflict. In F.M. Moghaddam, R. Harré, and N. Lee (Eds.), *Global Conflict Resolution through Positioning Analysis* (pp. 113–131). New York: Springer.

Lehecka, R., and Delbanco, A. (2007). Ivy-league let down. *The New York Times*, January 22, p. A21.

LeVine, R.A., and Campbell, D.T. (1972). *Ethnocentrism: Theories of Conflict, Ethnic Attitudes, and Group Behavior*. New York: John Wiley.

Locke, J. (1690/1948). Second treatise on civil government. In E. Barker (Ed.), *Social Contract: Essays by Locke, Hume, and Rousseau* (pp.1–143). London, UK: Oxford University Press.

Louis, W.R. and Taylor, D.M. (2004). Rights and duties as group norms: Implications of intergroup research for the study of rights and respon-sibilities. In N. Finkel and F.M. Moghaddam (Eds.), *The Psychology of Rights and Duties: Empirical Contributions and Normative Commen-taries* (pp. 105–134). Washington, D.C: American Psychological Association Press.

Mandaville, (2007). *Global Political Islam*. London, UK: Routledge.

Mann, C.C. (2006). *1491: New Revelations of the Americas Before Columbus*. New York: Knopf.

Marmot, M.G. (2004). *The Status Syndrome: How Social Standing Affects Our Health and Longevity*. New York: Times Books/Henry Holt.

Martin, G.B., and Clark, R.D. (1987). Distress crying in neonates: Species and peer specificity. *Developmental Psychology, 18*, 3–9.

Marx, K. (1852/1979). The eighteenth brumaire of Louis Bonaparte. In *Collected Works of Karl Marx and Frederick Engels* (vol. 11, pp. 99–197). London, UK: Lawrence Wishard.

Marx, K. and Engels, F. (1848/1967). *Communist Manifesto*. New York: Pantheon.

Masood, S. (2006). Pakistan's violent protests over cartoons taking political turn. *The New York Times*, February 13, p. A13.

McCarthy, M.P. and Campbell, S. (2001). *Security Transformation: Digital Defense Strategies to Protect Your Company's Reputation and Market Share*. New York: McGraw Hill.

Mearsheimer, J. and Walt, S. (2007). *The Israeli Lobby and U.S. Foreign Policy*. New York: Farrar, Straus & Giroux.

Meyer, B. and Geschiere, P. (Eds.) (1999). *Globalization and Identity: Dialectics of Flow and Closure*. Oxford, UK: Blackwell.

Meyers, N. and Kent, J. (2004). *The New Consumerism: The Influence of Affluence on the Environment*. Washington, DC: Island Press.

Moghaddam, F.M. (1994). Ethnic segregation in a multicultural society: A review of recent trends in Montreal and Toronto and reconceptualization of causal factors. In F. Frisken (Ed.), *The Changing Canadian Metropolis* (pp. 237–258). Berkeley, CA and Toronto, Ontario: University of California and Canadian Urban Studies Institute.

Moghaddam, F.M. (1997). *The Specialized Society: The Plight of the Individual in an Age of Individualism*. New York: Praeger.

Moghaddam, F.M. (1998). *Social Psychology: Exploring Universals Across Cultures*. New York: Freeman.

Moghaddam, F.M. (2002). *The Individual and Society: A Cultural and Historical Integration*. New York: Worth.

Moghaddam, F.M. (2003). Interobjectivity and Culture. *Culture and Psychology, 9*, 221–232.

Moghaddam, F.M. (2005). *Great Ideas in Psychology: A Cultural and Historical Introduction*. Oxford: Oneworld.

Moghaddam, F.M. (2006). Catastrophic evolution, culture and diversity management policy. *Culture & Psychology, 12*, 415–434.

Moghaddam, F.M. (2006). *From the Terrorists' Point of View: What They Experience and Why They Come to Destroy*. Westport, CT: Praeger Security International.

Moghaddam, F.M. (2007). Interrogation policy and American psychology in global context. *Peace and Conflict: Journal of Peace Psychology, 13*, 437–443.

Moghaddam, F.M. (2008). *Multiculturalism and Intergroup Relations: Psychological Implications for Democracy in Global Context*. Washington, DC: American Psychological Association Press.

Moghaddam, F.M. (In press). Religion and regional planning: The case of the emerging 'Shi'a Region'. In N. Slocum-Bradley (Ed.), *How Identity Constructions Promote Peace or Conflict*. London: Ashgate.

Moghaddam, F.M., and Kavulich, K.A. (2007). Nuclear positioning: The case of the Islamic Republic of Iran, The European Union, and the United States of America. In J. Valsiner and A. Rosa (Eds.), *The Cambridge Handbook of Sociocultural Psychology* (pp. 576–590). New York: Cambridge University Press.

Moghaddam, F. M., and Kavulich, K. A. (2008). Nuclear positioning and supererogatory duties: The illustrative case of positioning by Iran, the United States, and the European Union. In F.M. Moghaddam, R. Harré, and N. Lee (Eds.), *Global Conflict Resolution Through Positioning Analysis* (pp. 247–260). New York: Springer.

Moghaddam, F.M., and Riley, C.J. (2005). Toward a cultural theory of rights and duties in human development. In N. Finkel and F.M. Moghaddam (Eds.), *the Psychology of Rights and Duties: Empirical Contributions and Normative Commentaries* (pp. 74–104). Washington, DC: American Psychological Association Press.

Moghaddam, F.M. and Studer, C. (1998). *Illusions of Control: Striving for Control in Our Personal and Professional Lives*. Westport, CT: Praeger.

Murphy, C. (2008). Soldier of faith. *The Washington Post Magazine*, January 20, pp.16–20 and 27–29.

Myers, N. and Kent, J. (2004). *The New Consumers*. Washington, DC: Island Press.

Myrdal, G. (1944). *An American Dilemma: The Negro Problem and Modern Democracy*. (2 vols). New York: Harper and Bothers.

Nasre, V. (2006). *The Shi'a Revival: How Conflicts within Islam Will Shape the Future*. New York: Norton.

Nettle, D. and Romaine, S. (2000). *Vanishing Voices*. Oxford, UK: Oxford University Press.

Niemann, Y.F. and Maruyama, G. (2005). Inequalities in higher education. *Journal of Social Issues*, 61, 407–426.

Nugent, H. and Menuhin, N. (2007). Muhammad to top boys' names list. *The Times*, June 6, p. 8.

Oppel, R.A. (2008). Files for suicide bombers show no Down Syndrome. *The New York Times*, Feb 21, p. A6.

Osbeck, L., Moghaddam, F.M. and Perreault, S. (1997). Similarity and attraction among majority and minority groups in a multicultural context. *International Journal of Intercultural Relations*, 21, 113–123.

Oswald, D.L. (2006). Understanding anti-Arab reactions post 9/11: The role of threats, social categories, and personal ideologies. *Journal of Applied Social Psychology*, 35, 1775–1799.

Palmer, J.A. and Palmer, L.K. (2002). *Evolutionary Psychology: The Ultimate Origins of Human Behavior*. Boston, MA: Allyn & Bacon.

Perlez, J. (2007). Old church becomes mosque in altered and uneasy Britain. *The New York Times*, April 2, pp. A1 and A6.

Pettigrew, T. and Tropp, L.R. (2006). A meta-analytical test of intergroup contact theory. *Journal of Personality and Social Psychology*, 90, 751–783.

Popper, K. (1966). The open society and its enemies. New Jersey: Princeton University Press.

Postmes, T. and Jetten, J. (Eds.) (2006). *Individuality and the Group: Advances in Social Identity*. London, UK: Sage.

Putnam, R. (2000). *Bowling Alone: The Collapse of the Revival of American Community*. New York: Simon & Schuster.

Pyszczynski, T., Solomon, S., and Greenberg, J. (2003). *In the Wake of 9/11: The Psychology of Terror*. Washington, DC: American Psychological Association Press.

Reader, J. (1998). *Africa: Biography of the Continent*. New York: Knopf.

Reich, R.B. (2007). *Supercapitalism: The Transformatin of Business, Democracy and Everyday Life*. New York: Alfred A. Knopf.

Ritzer, G. (Ed.). *McDonaldization: The Reader*. Thousand Oaks, CA: Pine Forge Press.

Robertson, R. (1992). *Globalization: Social Theory and Global Culture*. London, UK: Sage.

Rothbart, D. and Korostelina, K.V. (Eds.) (2007). *Identity, Morality, and Threat: Studies in Violent Conflict*. New York: Lexington Books.

Rousseau, J.J. (1762/1997). *The Social Contract and Other Later Political Writings*. V. Gourevitch (Editor and translator). Cambridge, UK: Cambridge University Press.

Ruby, C.L. (2002). Are terrorists mentally deranged? *Analysis of Social Issues and Public Policy*, 2, 15–26.

Ruiz, G.M. and Carlton, J.T. (Eds.) (2004). *Invasive Species: Vectors and Management Strategies*. Washington, DC: Island Press.

Runciman, W.G. (1966). *Relative Deprivation and Social Justice*. Harmondsworth, UK: Penguin.

Ryan, L. (1981). *The Aboriginal Tasmanians*. St. Lucia: University of Queensland Press.

Sageman, M. (2004). *Understanding Terror Networks*. Pennsylvania, PA.: University of Pennsylvania Press.

Sageman, M. (2007). *Leaderless Jihad: Terror Networks in the Twenty-First Century*. Philadelphia, PA: University of Philadelphia Press.

Sakwa, R. (2008). *Putin: Russia's Choice*. London, UK: Routledge.

Shanker, T. and Fathi, N. (2008). Iran shows its own video of vessels' encounter in Gulf. *The New York Times*, Friday January 11, p. A3.

Shanker, T. and Knowlton, B. (2008). Iranian boats confront U.S. in Persian Gulf. *The New York Times*, Tuesday, January 8, pp. A1 and A4.

Sherif, M. (1966). *Group Conflict and Cooperation: Their Social Psychology*. London, UK: Routledge & Kegan Paul.

Sidanius, J. and Pratto, F. (1999). *Social Dominance: An Intergroup Theory of Social Dominance and Oppression*. Cambridge, UK: Cambridge University Press.

Skinner, B.F. (1948/1976). *Walden Two* (Revised edition). New York: Macmillan.

Skinner, B.F. (1971). *Beyond Freedom and Dignity*. New York: Macmillan.

Smallwood, S. (2003). American women surpass men in earning doctorates. *Chronicle of Higher Education*, December 12, p. A10.

Smith, A. (1776/1976). *An Inquiry into the Nature and Causes of the Wealth of Nations*. Vols 1 and 2. R.H. Campbell and A.S. Skinner (Eds.). London, UK: Oxford at the Clarendon Press.

Smith, C.S. (2007). French court rules for newspaper that printed Mohammad cartoons. *The New York Times*, March 23, p. A10.

Stephens, J.D. (1993). Capitalist development and democracy: Empirical research on the social origins of democracy. In D. Copp, J. Hampton, and J.E. Roemer (Eds.), *The Idea of Democracy* (pp. 409–446). New York: Cambridge University Press.

Sumner, W.G. (1906). *Folkways*. Boston, MA: Ginn.

Taylor, D.M. (2002). *The Quest for Identity*. Westport, CT: Praeger.

The New York Times (2008), The words that were used. January 29, p. A18.

Thomis, M.I. (1970). *The Luddites: Machine Breaking in Regency England*. Newton Abbot, UK.: David & Charles.

Thoreau, H.D. (1854/2003). *Walden and Civil Disobedience*. New York: Barnes and Noble Classics.

Tolstoy, L. (1869/1957). *War and Peace*. 2 vols. (R. Edmonds, translator). Harmondsworth, Middlesex: Penguin Classics.

Tolstoy, L. (1985). *Tolstoy's Diaries* (Edited and translated by R. F. Christian). vol. 1. 1847–1894. New York: Charles Scribner.

Trilling, L. (1971). *Sincerity and Authenticity*. Cambridge, MA: Harvard University Press.

Turnbull, C.M. (1972). *The Mountain People*. New York: Simon & Schuster.

Varga, C. (Ed.) (1992). *Comparative Legal Cultures*. New York: New York University Press.

Venter, J.C. et al., (2001). The sequence of the human genome. *Science, 291*, 1304–1351.

Vick, K. (2006). Iran's Khatami says Islam is the enemy West needs. *The Washington Post*, March 5, p. A17.

Waxman, S. (2007). "Pirates" haul so far estimated at $401 million. *The New York Times*, May 29, pp. B1, B8.

Wells, S. (2002). *The Journey of Man: A Genetic Odyssey*. Princeton, NJ: Princeton University Press.

Welsh, D. (1993). Domestic politics and ethnic conflict. In M.E. Brown (Ed.), *Ethnic Conflict and International Security* (pp. 43–60). Princeton, NJ: Princeton University Press.

Winslow, P.C. (2007). *Victory for Us Is to See You Suffer: In the West Bank with the Palestinians and the Israelis*. Boston, MA: Beacon Press.

Winter, D.G. (2003). Personality and political behavior. In D.O. Sears, L. Huddy, and R. Jervis (Eds.), *Oxford Handbook of Political Psychology* (pp. 111–145). Oxford, UK: Oxford University Press.

Wong, C. (2006). *Indicators for Urban and Regional Planning: The Interplay of Policy and Methods*. London: Routledge.

Yeats, W.B. (1962). *W.B. Yeats Selected Poetry* (ed. A.N. Jeffares). London: Macmillan.

Zangwill, I. (1909). *The Melting Pot: Drama in Four Acts*. New York: MacMillan.

Zimbardo, P. (2007). *The Lucifer Effect: Understanding How Good People Turn Evil*. New York: Random House.

NAME INDEX

SUBJECT INDEX

About the Author

FATHALI M. MOGHADDAM is Professor, Department of Psychology, and Director, Conflict Resolution Program, Department of Government, at Georgetown University and Senior Fellow at the Center for Interdisciplinary Policy, Education and Research on Terrorism. He has published extensively on the psychology of intergroup conflict, subjective justice, radicalization, and terrorism. The American Psychological Association's Society for the Study of Peace, Conflict and Violence awarded Dr. Moghaddam its 2007 Lifetime Achievement Award. His most recent books include *From the Terrorists' Point of View: What They Experience and Why They Come to Destroy* (Praeger Security International, 2006) and *Multiculturalism and Intergroup Relations: Psychological Implications for Democracy in Global Context* (2008).